The Durham Phenomenon

The Durham Phenomenon

TED HARRISON

Postscript by Rupert E. Davies

Darton, Longman and Todd
London

First published in 1985 by
Darton, Longman and Todd Ltd
89 Lillie Road, London SW6 1UD

ISBN 0 232 51671 5

British Library Cataloguing in Publication Data

Harrison, Ted
  The Durham phenomenon.
  1. Jenkins, David, *1925, Jan 26* — Contributions
in doctrinal theology   2. Theology, Doctrinal
  I. Title
  230′.092′4   BX5199.J3/

  ISBN 0–232–51671–5

Phototypeset by Input Typesetting Ltd, London
Printed and bound in Great Britain by
Anchor Brendon Ltd, Tiptree, Essex

Contents

Acknowledgements

My thanks are due to a number of people. To the staff of East Ward at the Kent and Canterbury Hospital who were very tolerant of a patient who insisted on finishing his book from a hospital bed. To John Newbury, Ronald Waters and my wife, Helen, for reading the manuscript and providing helpful suggestions. To Amanda de Winter who so gallantly typed the manuscript. And, of course, my thanks are due to David Jenkins himself for giving his time, providing transcripts of his sermons and articles and permitting me to quote from them. I should perhaps add that this is not a book authorized by the bishop who having read the manuscript neither lends his approval or disapproval to the book. My special thanks are due to Rupert E. Davies, former President of the Methodist Conference and Principal of Wesley College, Bristol, for adding a Postscript developing in more depth some of the theological implications of the 'Durham phenomenon' and for giving his specialist advice on the text generally.

Thanks are due to the following for permission to quote copyright material: the BBC for extracts from the 'Poles Apart' and 'Soundings' programmes and David Jenkins' Hibbert lecture; the Editor of the *Church Times*; the *Daily Telegraph*; London Weekend Television for the 'Credo' programme of 29 April 1984 in full and extracts from the 'Credo' programme of 16 March 1985; *Marxism Today*; SCM Press Ltd for extracts from David Jenkins' *The Contradiction of Christianity*.

TED HARRISON

1

A bolt of lightning

It was half past two in the morning on 9 July 1984. The thunder clouds which had gathered metaphorically over the Minster in York in the preceding weeks had taken physical form. Eye-witnesses spoke later of seeing a curious dancing light around the medieval church, others said they had seen bolts of lightning. What exactly happened no one will know except that the fire alarm connected to the Minster and installed in the fire-service headquarters sounded, the fire brigade rushed to the scene and found the Minster ablaze.

The ancient timbers at the southern end of the south transept roof had caught alight. Firemen described the burning building as being like a huge Roman candle; flames and sparks were soaring to the top of the two-hundred-foot tower. As the inferno raged, the oak vaulting – the product of years of faithful craftsmanship and recent restoration – smouldered, charred and turned to charcoal and ash. The glass in the irreplaceable windows cracked and the lead buckled and melted with the heat.

As firemen began to play huge jets of water on the blaze, the city of York started to come to life. The smoke, the noise and the orange glow in the sky roused the friends of the Minster and the clergy, many of whom immediately offered their services to help rescue the Minster treasures. Priceless altar cloths, carpets, candlesticks and crosses were carried to the safety of houses nearby until firemen ordered volunteers to stop their work as pieces of burning wood began to fall from the roof along with droplets of molten lead.

When dawn broke it became clear that the roof of the south transept was completely destroyed. First estimates were that it would cost over a million pounds to repair. But it also became apparent that, apart from water and smoke damage, the bulk of the Minster was unharmed. The windows too had suffered less damage than at first had been feared. The famous sixteenth-century rose window, consisting of eight thousand individual panes painted by craftsmen from the Low Countries, was most affected, but even that was not beyond repair. It had been re-leaded and strengthened only fifteen years before.

Later that same day when the Archbishop of Canterbury visited the scene he noted the damage with sadness but added the thoughts shared by many, 'It seems miraculous that the fire was so confined and the problem is contained within the roof. The Minster will rise again.'

There were others however who talked of a miracle of a different kind. Was the hand of a judgemental God at work? Had the lightning strike been a sign from above? Was God displeased with his Church? Was he saddened by the fact that three days earlier the Minster had been the venue for the consecration as bishop of a man regarded by a body of traditional opinion as a heretic? Clouds of controversy and theological passion had gathered in York on the day Professor David Jenkins became a bishop. On the third day after, the elements unleashed their destructive power.

2

Donning the mitre

The Archangel Gabriel must be killing himself with laughter, David Jenkins is reported to have said on his appointment to the See of Durham. He had, he explained, just been helping run a course for new bishops, because of 'the impossible things they have to do nowadays', and now a bishopric had come his way.

The bishops of the Church of England, the established Church, are chosen in a curious way. Theirs is a quasi-political appointment in that the committee of church dignitaries, the Crown Appointments Commission, which recommends names cannot confirm its own recommendations. It submits two names to the Prime Minister who then recommends one of the nominees to the Queen for preferment or asks for two more names. The bishop-designate must then be elected by the Dean and Chapter of the cathedral where there is the vacancy, and the Chapter is legally bound to accept the name the Queen puts forward. While the Crown Appointments Commission is a relatively new body (prior to 1977 bishops were chosen by a mysterious system of selection known only to 'number 10 Downing Street' and a handful of initiates), the election procedure is steeped in history and ecclesiastical law.

The Bishop of Durham is the fourth most senior bishop in the Anglican Church – after the Archbishops of Canterbury and York and the Bishop of London. As one of the top five diocesan bishoprics it carries with it an automatic seat in the House of Lords. The other diocesan bishops have to wait for one of the remaining twenty-one seats on the Bench of Bishops in the Upper House to become vacant before enjoying the privilege of being a 'Lord Spiritual'.

While most newly appointed diocesan bishops would expect to have served as a suffragan, or assistant, bishop prior to enthronement, appointments to the See of Durham have often proved exceptions to the rule. The Bishop of Durham is often a man distinguished as an academic, thrust from university life to a senior episcopal appointment in one move. Dr John Habgood, who was leaving the diocese to become Archbishop of York, was Principal of Queen's College, Birmingham, before becoming a bishop.

So it was in keeping with that tradition that the Queen, on the advice of the Prime Minister and on the recommendation of a team of senior bishops and diocesan representatives, asked David Jenkins, Professor of Theology at Leeds University and joint Director of the William Temple Foundation, to forsake the world of learning for the pomp, pastoral responsibilities and bureaucracy of the life of a diocesan bishop. David Jenkins was already nearly sixty, approaching an age when many in secular life are considering retirement or at least thinking that the major part of their life is over, when he was asked to take up a new challenge. The appointment was made public on 14 March 1984.

In view of what has been said by many people later, it is interesting to note that when the appointment was made public there were no howls of protest from any quarter. To those who knew him as a theologian, as a teacher or preacher, he would have been considered an orthodox liberal thinker, prepared to be provocative, but not in any way out of place in the Anglican Church. On his appointment the *Church Times* said he 'has been described as an "open theologian" '. But he had no public image, as modern biblical scholarship was not a popular pursuit. Indeed, as the subsequent debate was to demonstrate, the ordinary church-goer was largely unaware of the currency,

4

let alone the subtleties, of the contemporary theological debate. As for the mass of lay opinion, the debate was beyond ken and comprehension.

David Edward Jenkins was born on 26 January 1925 into an 'ordinary middle-class' family.

'My childhood was very happy in a quiet sort of way, not given to rows, and with a great deal of affection – one which has left me with a sense of security and thankfulness and pleasant memories. No periods of great stress.

'My father was an insurance inspector. He worked for the Scottish Providence Society. My grandfather had been a lay preacher and a master carpenter. My mother was a rather up-stage Wesleyan and my father was a more down-market Primitive.' Methodism was therefore the family denomination and from an early age chapel-going and Sunday School were for the growing David an integral part of life.

'I remember getting rather fed up with Methodist Sunday School around the age of nine, thinking that I was being treated in too much of a childish fashion. But then, aged plus or minus ten, I started attending the Crusader classes. That is when, from the point of view of a developing faith, things began to be in any way memorable. I found myself as one of a group of persons who seemed to me to be getting onto something by regularly exploring the Bible and swapping insights about texts and so on. I became part of a group which studied the Bible and had prayer meetings. People have tended to say I was a fairly precocious ten-year-old.

'I don't think I can remember a time when I didn't assume that what I was being taught I was also exploring. We discussed everything.

'There was a Bible-class leader and I have the picture – I can see it now in my mind's eye – of him sitting there and the class sitting round, and we all had our Bibles open and we were all discussing. Questioning was always for me a positive thing – exploring. It was taken for granted but within a very firm framework of faith. We were offered various lectures and harangues. It was all very evangelical. We assumed that the Bible was the word of God in some simple sense, but the way you got onto that was by your exploring it.

'I am aware that there was an assumption that everything one did was of interest to God, and should be in accordance with God's will, and so we were encouraged to pray what we called arrow prayers. In the middle of something you would remember God and address a message to him, or wonder if you had a message from him. Certainly one was encouraged in self-examination, and of course that got picked up when I went from the evangelical classes via the evangelical Church of England to the catholic side of the Church of England. This was when I was fourteen or fifteen. The basis of it all was that you were a sinner and needed saving; somehow the positive side struck me more than the negative, and I don't remember pangs of guilt or worrying unduly, though I did have the sense of God being immediately present if needed.'

David Jenkins went to school at St Dunstan's College, Catford. It was a local Anglo-Catholic curate in Newport Pagnall who befriended him in his formative years as a teenager and broadened his view of Christianity. 'I never went through a stage of rejecting my faith. One is supposed to be rebellious in youth but I don't remember that in my case. In theory I should be surprised at that.'

David Jenkins' teens were of course dominated by the Second World War. He left home earlier than he might otherwise have done, being evacuated to Reigate in Surrey to avoid the bombing of London. Indeed the family home was partly destroyed in one attack. Lionel and Dora Jenkins, his parents, were in the house at the time but were fortunately unhurt. The front of the house was blown in while they were in a back room.

To David and his younger brother the war was a time of excitement.

'I remember seeing planes flying overhead and, being plane spotters, we were able to identify them. I was a more phlegmatic person than my brother and took things in my stride, adapting school life to sharing with a school in Reigate, digging trenches and just getting on with it. The thing I remember most was listening to the news of the fall of France on the radio and getting both a very strong sinking feeling about that and the realization that the war would almost certainly go on long enough for me to be in it.

'It wasn't an idea I was looking forward to, but it wasn't something I thought I shouldn't do. However lively my faith, issues of pacifism just didn't enter my head.'

The young David Jenkins joined the army in 1943 at the age of eighteen. At school he had been a senior sergeant in the Officer Training Corps and he was familiar with much he was to come across in the early days of military service. 'Everybody was involved in some way in the war, I just got on with what I had to do. The O.T.C. had got me used to discipline and given me a head start in learning about the Bren gun. I knew some of the first moves.'

After his initial training with the Suffolks, David Jenkins was sent to Glasgow University on a six-month course to become an officer in the Royal Artillery.

'I can't think what the point of it was. We did a lot of military training with the University O.T.C. and did courses at the University on elementary engineering and explosives.

'I was commissioned very close to V.E. Day. In fact I was on a firing camp at Otterburn on V.E. Day.'

A year later he was sent to India, where he was for two years. He rose to the rank of Captain but was never called into action. In March 1947 he became due for some home leave but decided instead to use the time exploring the Himalayas. He travelled from Calcutta to Darjeeling, to Sikkim and the Tibetan border.

'I developed an appreciation of the awesomeness of God, and that which goes from awesomeness to glory. It struck me too, in a different way, going south with the regiment to a cholera-stricken area. It was all part of the mystery. There were people dying and there was an uncertainty, a mystery about things. It became clearer to me that things were not as simple as I might have thought once.'

His army experience did not however shake his belief that he would one day seek ordination. 'My faith had come alive during the Crusader classes and by the time I was a young teenager I assumed I had some particular call, and this would probably be to the priesthood. This was when I was thirteen or fourteen.'

First, however, David Jenkins took up the scholarship he had been awarded in his last year at school and went to Queen's College, Oxford. For most of the next twenty years Queen's College was to be his life, and that of his wife Mollie, whom he married in 1949. First of all he took a Second in both Mods and Greats, graduating as a Bachelor of Arts in 1951. He stayed on at Oxford for an additional year to take a First in Theology. From Lincoln Theological College he was ordained deacon in 1953 and priest a year later. For a year he lectured at Queen's College, Birmingham, and was the succentor (a junior clerical member of staff) at the Cathedral.

However, he was to spend only two years away from Oxford. In 1954 he took up an appointment as Fellow, Chaplain and Praelector in Theology at his old college. Over the next fifteen years David Jenkins' reputation as an academic was to become established. In 1955 he became a lecturer in theology at Oxford and as the years passed, became examining chaplain to the bishops of a number of dioceses. As a sign of his academic distinction he was in 1966 asked to deliver the Bampton Lectures. These lectures are given under the terms of the will of a certain Canon John Bampton who directed that 'eight divinity lecture sermons shall be preached upon either of the following subjects, to conform and establish the Christian Faith, and to confute all heretics and schismatics: upon the divine authority of the Holy Scriptures; upon the authority of the writings of the Primitive Fathers, as the faith and practice of the Primitive Church; upon the Divinity of our Lord and Saviour Jesus Christ; upon the Divinity of the Holy Ghost; upon the articles of the Christian Faith, as comprehended in the Apostles' and Nicene Creeds.' The Heads of the Oxford colleges were obliged under the terms of the will to select a lecturer who would not deviate from a standard interpretation of the Anglican faith.

He was known at Queen's both as 'a man who talked so fast that his contemporaries were inclined to believe he must be very clever' and as 'a bit of a windbag, though a lively and interesting one. A theologian who said a lot which didn't add up.'

In 1969 David Jenkins left academic life to become Director of the 'Humanum' study for the World Council of Churches in Geneva. The subject of the study was the whole situation of man in the light of the Christian faith. This took him to Australia, the United States and the Middle East and after four years he returned to Britain to become Director of the William Temple Foundation, now part of the Manchester Business School. From 1979 he combined this appointment with the Chair in Theology and Religious Studies at Leeds University, and for a while he shared the editorship of *Theology*.

David Jenkins is a man of average build, most noticeable for his shock of white hair and animated way of talking.

The lawyer, writer and well-known sceptic John Mortimer wrote this description of his visit to Bishop Auckland Castle to see the controversial prelate:

> Sitting in an armchair, he thought with his entire body. When momentarily flummoxed he would throw his small, brightly-shod feet into the air and lie almost prone in silent thought. When the words came pouring out, as they often did, he sat eagerly, his fingers ticking off points against each other.

David Jenkins admits to a love of Maigret novels, reading them in French for 'the smell of Paris', and to an incongruous enjoyment of the book by Jim Corbett called *Man-Eaters of Kumaon* about tiger-hunting in India. However, David Jenkins' greatest pleasure is music, Verdi and Mozart in particular. He quotes the Swiss theologian Karl Barth on the subject, 'If Mozart's not in heaven, I'm not going to stay.'

When David Jenkins was appointed Bishop the powers that be in the Church had no cause to suspect that the choice would prove to be so controversial. He had all the right qualifications to be a good, unremarkable bishop, with perhaps the ability to ginger up the thinking faithful but certainly none of the hallmarks of a man of mass appeal. At Christmas in 1984, less than a year after his appointment, he reflected somewhat ruefully on what had befallen him. Writing in *The Observer* newspaper he mused:

> When I was a boy we had crackers at Christmas and the crackers always had riddles in them. If God were to design a cracker for me this Christmas, I suspect that the riddle would read something like this, 'When is an accident providential?'
>
> So far as I was concerned it was simply accidental that I should be asked on a TV programme about miracles, and therefore about the virgin birth and the resurrection

of Jesus, at a moment when I was not only a professor of theology but also a bishop-designate.

I was on the programme, so I understood, because I was known to be a theologian familiar with, and sympathetic to, modern critical ways of thinking who, none the less, combined this with a commitment to orthodox Christian faith, built round a traditional understanding of God as the Holy Trinity and Jesus Christ as the man who was God. As the critical position I was stating has been in wide circulation for something up to one hundred years and reflects questions which have been discussed for over two hundred years, and as the form of my Christian faith is, probably, unusually traditional and orthodox among scholars and intellectuals, it never occurred to me that anyone would be interested in my answer, let alone excited by it.

However, the response to the programme, broadcast on 29 April 1984, was so great that not only was the 'Bishop of Durham issue' to become the dominant topic of discussion in church circles but theology was to escape from the confines of the colleges and cities of dreaming spires and become a matter of wide public debate.

3

'I wouldn't put it past God . . . but'

'Credo' is a London Weekend Television production transmitted nationally in Britain, formerly on the Independent Television network, but now on Channel 4. Although it is transmitted on Saturday evenings, its origins can be traced to the 'God slot', a period during the early Sunday evening schedule, when companies felt obliged to transmit religious programmes.

Religious broadcasting in Britain stretches back to the very early days of the radio when the British Broadcasting Corporation was set up and put in the care of the formidable and austere Presbyterian, John Reith. He set as one of his priorities the responsible transmission of the Christian faith by the new medium in his charge.

As the years passed, and as broadcasting became more sophisticated and television overtook radio as the chief medium of electronic man's communication, simple acts of worship, epilogues and homilies were no longer considered adequate. Religious documentaries, modelled on those dealing with current affairs, were produced. Church news and theological matters were no longer handled with undue reverence. Journalists and news producers took an interest in the subjects once reserved for learned articles and pulpits, and they began to ask searching questions from a lay perspective. The pattern was pioneered by the BBC Radio 4 programme 'Sunday'. In the 1970s the distinguished and vastly experienced BBC news correspondent Gerald Priestland became Religious Affairs Correspondent and added considerable personal weight to the news interest in matters religious. Religious stories became increasingly judged by the yardsticks of general news coverage.

The television age also heralded the era of the 'pop scholar' – academics who had a gift for communication on the small two-dimensional screen. There was Sir Mortimer Wheeler, the archaeologist; Professor A. J. P. Taylor, the historian; Dr Magnus Pyke, the nutritionist; Patrick Moore, who brought new popularity to the study of astronomy; as did Alec Clifton-Taylor to architecture.

The 'Credo' programme brought these two trends together. It decided to tackle the issues of current theological scholarship as news involving various academics chosen both for their position on the spectrum of opinion and their ability to communicate. If the same team had been making a political documentary they would have followed a similar approach, finding good speakers from Left and from Right and a good standard man or woman in the middle. For the 'Credo' programme Professor Jenkins was considered to be of sufficient standing and authority, to be of balanced views and to be a good talker. An ideal middle man. It was not the first programme of this type. It had been preceded, in particular, by a production called 'Jesus: the Evidence', a dissection of the gospel stories using historical and scientific analytical techniques.

Since the original 'Credo' interview, on 29 April 1984, was instrumental in launching the 'Durham affair' and since there have been so many claims that the Bishop was misquoted or quoted out of context, it is as well to report the programme extensively. As the bishop-elect was to learn, the spoken word, especially delivered on television with explanatory gestures and facial expressions, does not translate readily into print. Allowance should be made for this if some of the quoted passages appear difficult to follow as reproduced on the page. The presenter was Phillip Whitehead, one of the school of television journalists with

13

a keen interest in religious matters, trained and grounded in politics and current affairs. The interview with David Jenkins was unscripted and some sections are difficult to follow because of their off-the-cuff nature.

PHILLIP WHITEHEAD: Jesus has been worshipped by Christians down the ages as the divine being who had come to earth to save mankind.

But now, key elements of the story of Jesus as the Son of God are seen by some Christians themselves as legends rather than the historical truth.

So how does the Church reconcile the new view of the Gospels with the vision of Jesus it has preached for hundreds of years?

Religion is above all a matter of faith. But as the vehement reaction among Christians to the recent TV series on the evidence concerning the life of Jesus has shown, for many religious people, faith in the truth of what their sacred texts tell them is extremely important.

However, the more miraculous the accounts of the life of the founder of a religion, the more vulnerable they will appear in an age of doubt such as ours. And Christianity, the most widespread of all religions, would also seem the most vulnerable among the major religions on this count.

The reason for this is the same as the chief reason why Christianity has proved the most powerful religion in history. It is that the claims made on behalf of its founder have been the most striking of all.

At the heart of Christianity lies the idea that in Jesus, God took human form. It has traditionally defined Christians' views of God, of Jesus, and of themselves as believers. They have called themselves Christians because they see Christ as the Saviour of Mankind. He died on the cross to pay for man's original sin, replacing the prospect of eternal damnation for all with the hope of salvation through repentance.

But his act of atonement has gained its real significance

from being seen not just as the death of a man, but as God's self-sacrifice. It's through this supreme demonstration of love that God has revealed himself to Christians as not only just but also full of mercy.

STEWART SUTHERLAND (author of *God, Jesus and Belief*): Christians believe that men and women are sinners, they believe that we are flawed and weak. They believe also that we cannot save ourselves. Fortunately they can also believe, as Christians, that God came down to earth and that, in Jesus Christ, he provided the means of saving them from this state. Through his redeeming work, through his work on the cross, through his sacrifice on the cross, they have the possibility of being saved and forgiven.

PHILLIP WHITEHEAD: The idea that the death of Jesus amounts to God's self-sacrifice has traditionally been reinforced by the miraculous details of Jesus's life as recorded in the Gospels.

His life starts with a miracle – his conception in the womb of a virgin who was told by the Angel Gabriel that she had been made pregnant by the Holy Ghost. He goes through life performing miracles, such as feeding five thousand people with a few fishes and loaves of bread. But, most important, after his death he rises again and appears among his disciples as a living person of flesh and blood.

All this has been seen as evidence that he was God incarnate.

RICHARD HANSON (former Professor of Theology, Manchester University): From the beginning, almost from the beginning, certainly from the first or second century A.D., practically all the Christian thinkers took the fact that Jesus was supposed to have been born from a virgin, that he did miracles, especially miracles like walking on water and turning water into wine, and that he rose from the dead as the sign that he was divine, not simply human but also divine.

PHILLIP WHITEHEAD: But Christians haven't just insisted that Jesus was divine. They have at the same time clung fast to the notion that though he was God he was also fully a man. And while his divinity has been crucial to the idea that through his death he paid for the sins of mankind, his humanity has helped to give the Christian faith its unique power among the religions of the world.

DENNIS NINEHAM (Professor of Theology, Bristol University): One of the most distinctive characteristics of Christianity and, I suspect, one that has given it a very large part of its attraction has been the idea that in Christ, God personally and fully identified himself with mankind, with the human lot, and with all its miseries and imperfections and fears, and so on. This has helped people in the midst of all those fears and troubles enormously and it's also given them a sense of great closeness to God and the feeling that they could be one with him in the sort of way in which he had been, become one with them in the person of Christ, and you can't have a closer union than that.

PHILLIP WHITEHEAD: The idea of Jesus as both God and man, and the truth of the miraculous details of his story in the gospels, went largely unquestioned for hundreds of years. But more recently there's been a dramatic change. The advance of science has inspired in people a new way of looking at the world, in which the idea of miracles and divine intervention has no place. This has led many of them to reject religion completely, and has inspired in many others doubts about its full validity.

But it has also had an effect on Christian theologians; especially in the Protestant churches. The majority of them have tried to reinterpret the story of Jesus in a way that makes sense to the twentieth-century mind.

Theologians who may differ on the other matters, now agree on seeing many of the miracles as not a record of what actually happened. Instead, they regard them as stories attached to Jesus by the early Christians after his death, to express their faith in him as the Messiah. Some have gone further. They apply the new approach not only to the miracles, but to the resurrection itself.

KEITH WARD (Professor of Moral Theology, King's College, London): Some theologians think that Jesus didn't actually appear after his death to the apostles, but as they were so shocked by his death and knew the great significance his life had had, they believed that this could not simply end, and they put their belief in a story form about appearances. But what it really meant for them was that they were explaining his life by saying that its significance and value could not end but was going on living for ever, so that Jesus in a sense was always with them, even to the end of the world.

PHILLIP WHITEHEAD: But that's not all. A number of theologians have gone on to question the very idea that Jesus was both God and man. They say that in the first place it detracts from the power of Jesus's story. To see him as God makes his anguish, his famous cry on the cross, 'My God, My God, why have you forsaken me?' and his death itself seem unreal. For as God he would have known his fate in advance, including his certain resurrection.

But more important, these theologians argue, in twentieth-century terms the idea that he was both God and man just doesn't make sense.

MAURICE WILES (Regius Professor of Divinity, Oxford University): For me there is a problem of the logical coherence of that traditional doctrine which speaks of Jesus as a single person who's both fully human and also fully God, because to be fully human is, it seems to me, to be a particular individual who has emerged at a particular point in history with a particular genetic inheritance, who makes decisions from his limited growing human knowledge, whereas the traditional understanding of God is to be one who is eternal, the creator of everything that is, and omniscient. And to say that Jesus is fully human but also that he's personally God, the incarnation of the second person of the Trinity, with those characteristics, does seem to me to pose a real problem.

PHILLIP WHITEHEAD: These theologians realize if Jesus is not seen as God, then the crucifixion can no longer be regarded as God's self-sacrifice to pay for the sins of mankind. And this inevitably undermines the traditional idea of Jesus as the Redeemer, and of the redemption itself.

But these radical theologians say it's not necessary to see Jesus as God to retain faith in salvation. For they see what happened on the cross not as a once-and-for-all payment for man's original sin, but only as the most special example of the mercy which a loving God continually extends to his children. And they see Jesus acting in this, as throughout his life, not as God, but as a human being used by God to speak to mankind.

MAURICE WILES: For me Jesus is distinctive and unique because I see him as a human person supremely responsive and open to the spirit of God and thereby able to express the character of God and to effect God's action in the world, in an absolutely distinctive way. And I think this enables us to say most of the things that Christians have been insisting on in speaking of Jesus as God, while seeing him more intelligibly perhaps as a responsive human person rather than in the traditional sense as in his own person and actually the second person of the Trinity, God himself.

PHILLIP WHITEHEAD: But of course, the views of theologians on Jesus are one thing. The views of ordinary Christians on him are something else, especially when it comes to the idea of Jesus's divinity.

Indeed, the results of a special poll done for 'Credo' by the Harris Research Centre suggests that, on this issue, the views of radical theologians conflict not only with those of churchgoers, but with the views of most people in the country as a whole.

In our poll, of the total sample asked whether Jesus was the Son of God or just a man, 52 per cent said he was the Son of God and only 24 per cent that he was just a man. 16 per cent said that they didn't know and 8 per cent that he had never existed.

When it came to regular churchgoers, 78 per cent said that Jesus was the Son of God, and only 13 per cent that he was just a man. 6 per cent said they didn't know, and 3 per cent that he had never existed.

Between the churchgoers and the theologians stands the Church itself. It is to the leaders of the Church that believers look for guidance. Indeed, the view which the Church takes of Jesus in this age of doubt is likely to be of interest to a large number of unbelievers as well.

So, to get an idea of what leading churchmen think, earlier this week we interviewed one of the most prominent biblical scholars among the leaders of the Church of England, the Reverend Professor, David Jenkins, recently appointed the Bishop of Durham.

Professor Jenkins, do churchmen like you hold the view that miraculous details of the story of Jesus, like his birth to a virgin or the fact that he walked on the water, ought to be taken as representing the literal truth today?

DAVID JENKINS: No, but I think it's important to make some distinctions. There's a distinction, it seems to me, between miracles which are events which seem to happen when people are getting excited about important matters and which raise wonder, so I think it quite likely that Jesus performed miracles or was thought to perform miracles.

And then there's the question of telling miraculous stories because you've already had a wonderful belief, and I think the virgin birth is like that – I mean, to show people really believed that he came from God and all the rest of it, they told the story of the virgin birth, And then there's finally the resurrection which I think is a whole different kettle of fish, but I expect you'll come to that.

PHILLIP WHITEHEAD: Could you just tell me, what you would understand then by Jesus performing miracles in the sense you've just used there?

DAVID JENKINS: I don't really know, but I mean I am quite aware that miracles seem to happen, I mean across the world, and not necessarily in connection with Christianity. That is to say, that when there is a certain sort of religious excitement, charismatic experience and commitment, things happen such as healings, which look contrary to ordinary nature and so on, and the issue then is, well, are they just an interesting phenomenon or are they part of something else? But then miracles are strictly things that make you wonder, and the question then is how do you answer the source of this wonder?

PHILLIP WHITEHEAD: Yes, I can see that with the miracles which relate to healing, and it is more difficult to follow that into the story of the virgin birth or into the story of Jesus walking on the water. Do you see those as in the same category?

DAVID JENKINS: Well, no I don't actually. I think the walking on the water one is very difficult and after all there are stories about Tibetan holy men being able to do quite remarkable things, so I just have an open mind on that.

The virgin birth, I'm pretty clear is a story told after the event in order to express and symbolize a faith that this Jesus was a unique event from God, you see, so it's different from the other miracles in my view and I mean, if I might be allowed to say so, I wouldn't put it past God to arrange a virgin birth if he wanted but I very much doubt if he would, because it seems contrary to the way in which he deals with persons and brings his wonders out of natural personal relationships.

Yes, yes, the birth narratives for instance, which I think they look like legends as you call them, I think they are the basis of them, there is of course already believing that Jesus is a unique person who's come uniquely from God, and then you symbolize that by drawing on material that's available to you from what we call the Old Testament, because of course he has fulfilled that pattern so you find other details and you probably read into it things from the Hellenistic world which you're part of.

PHILLIP WHITEHEAD: So they don't amount to a historical record and shouldn't be seen as such, but as a series of stories to emphasize the unique importance of Jesus.

DAVID JENKINS: Yes, and the belief already held, that is what I . . . yes, I think so.

PHILLIP WHITEHEAD: Could we move on then now to the most important miracle in the whole story of Jesus, the story of the resurrection. Do you hold the view that Jesus rose from the dead and ascended into heaven?

DAVID JENKINS: Well, I hold the view that he rose from the dead. The question is what that means, isn't it? I would like to say that I don't think the resurrection is *a* miracle – that is to say, that it doesn't seem to me, reading the records as they remain in both the Gospels and what Paul says in 1 Corinthians, that there was any one event which you could identify with the resurrection. What seems to me to have happened is that there were a series of experiences which convinced, gradually convinced, a growing number of the people who became apostles that Jesus had certainly been dead, certainly buried and he wasn't finished, and what is more he wasn't just not finished but he was raised up, that is to say, the very life and power and purpose and personality which was in him was actually continuing, and was continuing both in the sphere of God and in the sphere of history, so that he was a risen and living presence and possibility.

PHILLIP WHITEHEAD: But could that faith be an internally experienced thing on their part, in the sense that sometimes when a death has moved us greatly, and here is the death of a very, very remarkable person, we sense the bereaved in our bereavement. We sense a presence still with us?

DAVID JENKINS: I myself believe that it was more than that, that is to say that it wasn't a question of people making up things out of their wishes however sincerely, but that this was part of the way in which God does communicate with people, that he puts himself into personal and internal events so that there was more of a cause to it than just my imagination or Paul's imagination or Peter's imagination. That God was somehow involved in producing this event. So if you'd like to call that a miracle, okay.

PHILLIP WHITEHEAD: So you're talking about a literal apparition, a manifestaton?

DAVID JENKINS: Well there were . . . there must have been some as it were quasi-physical, quasi-psychological causes, but of course whether that really meant that what God had been doing in Jesus he was going on doing until the end of the world, was something you had to bet your life on, I mean obviously you can't get that out of the experience just as such. It has to grow up into a communal faith.

PHILLIP WHITEHEAD: If I can come on now to perhaps the

most important question of all, that is whether Jesus was both God and Man or, as some theologians I think would now argue, a man divinely appointed acting as God's agent. Would you say, as in the case of the resurrection, we don't have the evidence to be absolutely sure on that point?

DAVID JENKINS: Clearly we don't – I mean I don't – know what would be evidence to make you absolutely sure on that point. It's the question of the way the understanding and the faith of the Church built up and I think it starts from the identification which distinguished Christians from Jews, which is that Jesus was God's Messiah, . . . something like God's final act or final agent. God is going to do something which will finally wind things up and fulfil his Kingdom and he's going to do it via his Messiah. And the resurrection which we've been talking about convinced the disciples that this Jesus, this crucified man, was God's Messiah. So that made him in some sense God's last work, the way in which God would finally act to bring in his Kingdom of Love and all the rest of it. And now, if he was God's last work, this gave him a unique relationship to God, and the belief built up . . . and when this was worked out in Greek terms – which was the way people thought about reality then – then the way of saying this was in fact what we've actually got, not God just doing it through him, but God doing it *as* him. So that there's a sense in which we have to re-understand God. God is not just transcendent and beyond everything, and doesn't just work through other agents, but he has so much love and is so down-to-earth that you can actually believe that there was a real sense in which God is Jesus and Jesus is God.

PHILLIP WHITEHEAD: What do you say to the people who are puzzled by the degree to which you are prepared to allow a large part of the early story of Jesus to be a wonderful extended poetic metaphor perhaps? But you seem to me to be saying that what was arrived at four hundred and fifty years later does have to be taken on a very different level.

DAVID JENKINS: No, because I think that poetry has its own logic and is referring to its reality, and the poetic witness to Jesus in the story of the virgin birth is about exactly the same thing, and the poetry has got to be lived out into the down-to-earthness now. I think we've only got, as it were, two places where you can come up against the reality, and one is in occasional experiences of something like mysticism – prayer that seems to take you beyond yourself into a reality which you only call God, and the other is when you're trying to take seriously your life now, your relationship now, for instance how you use the environment now, and so on. This is the story that I'm living by, this is the story that I think will come true. And so this is the story in which I put my hope and faith and practice.

PHILLIP WHITEHEAD: But isn't that a story which could be equally important, potent, if it was a story of the realization of the work of Jesus as a man?

DAVID JENKINS: I think that there isn't the least doubt that people have felt this magnetic attraction of Jesus and get on to the wavelength in all sorts of ways. I think, however, that the Church has a responsibility of keeping alive this sort of defining demand about it. That's why I think the creeds should go on being said in Church. They symbolize in a language which can be worked out this claim, how you make the claim – and after all, lots of people who recite the creeds don't live up to it, just as lots of people who can't recite the creeds do. But there is this particular purpose of keeping this possibility alive and saying, are you really sure that, in reinterpreting in this way, you've done full justice to the possibilities of the world which are the possibilities of God?

PHILLIP WHITEHEAD: Can you understand the point of view of people who say, 'Well, I hear what you say, I can understand it, and I see at this point in historical time, A.D. 451, all of the reasons why the early Fathers of the Church formulated the creed, said what they said at that time, but as a twentieth-century, more rational man, I can't see that, and you're not making a sufficient adjustment into my twentieth-century pattern of thought.'?

DAVID JENKINS: Yes, well clearly that's the sort of argument that should be kept open. I'm not always convinced that twentieth-century man is much more rational, he's just rational in different ways, and I think we're beginning to discover that a whole lot of openness is required. I think there are two things really. I think what I want to insist on is that, one, the argument will be kept open because that's what I understand God is about — openness, transcendence, always more — and secondly, that it is clear that the argument is actually about God and only in one sense, secondarily, about Jesus. I mean, what are the wavelengths which are open to us now that we can get on to, which are pointed to by this original impact of Jesus by the records in the New Testament and by all the arguments that had gone on? So carry on with the arguments, but don't let either of us give in, and see where we get to.

I mean — wanting to put into modern terms the splendid phrase that Augustine used, which is that 'dogmas are fence round the mystery' — if you go too far that way you know nothing but man. Listen, look inwards. I think you certainly can't have the sort of definiteness, the sort of precision which for a long time people have believed. That's wrong, I think.

PHILLIP WHITEHEAD: So you wouldn't want to see any ring fence put round the Church and its teaching on the basis of the issue we've discussed today?

DAVID JENKINS No, but if somebody said to me, I don't think Jesus is anything to do with God and there isn't a God, well then I don't think he ought to be in the Church.

PHILLIP WHITEHEAD: No, but if he says, I believe passionately in Jesus as a great moral teacher and a divine agent and he's leading me towards God, but I don't believe that he was God-made-flesh, is he still a Christian?

DAVID JENKINS: Oh yes, yes.

PHILLIP WHITEHEAD Thank you very much. So it seems that for churchmen like the Bishop-elect of Durham, precise dogmas about Jesus are a thing of the past. All are open to argument, if not reinterpretation.

Within this, the main thing to understand about the disputed details of Jesus's story and of views about him, is that they all are rooted in faith.

Accounts of his birth to a virgin and of such miracles as his walking on water, are expressions of the early Christians' faith in Jesus as the Messiah. The resurrection was not a single event, but a series of experiences on the part of his disciples and followers, linked together by their faith in Jesus into the conviction that he was alive among them. And the idea that Jesus was God grew gradually among the early Christians out of their belief that, in Jesus, God had become manifest as not only transcendent, but at work in the world around them.

Churchmen like Professor Jenkins stand by the idea of Jesus as God because of their faith, nourished by personal experience, of God's close involvement in the world, of which they see Jesus as the ultimate revelation. However, instead of casting out those who regard Jesus not as God but as a mortal human being acting as God's agent, churchmen like the Bishop-elect of Durham are prepared to welcome them as Christians. And that's a big change indeed for the Church of England.

Phillip Whitehead's summary and closing remarks were wrong in one respect. What the Bishop-elect had said did not involve a big change for the Anglican Church. It may well have been rare for such doctrinal tolerance to have been aired by such a senior churchman to a general television audience, but the ideas themselves were well established in the theological colleges and university faculties of divinity.

To the lay person, on first hearing, some of the Bishop-elect's views would have been clear enough; certainly those concerning the virgin birth. Other ideas would have appeared more obscure, and Professor Jenkins did not help matters with his muddled delivery. But he admits the English language is a very inadequate tool when it comes to explaining matters eternal. 'I am no poet,' he once said, 'I wish that I were.'

In that there is no ready and easily accessible style of speech to describe concepts theological to the lay person, Professor Jenkins employed an uneasy mix of lecture-hall jargon and colloquialisms. He largely failed in his first attempt to explain what he understood by the resurrection and although in later interviews and sermons he was to clarify his view, the 'Credo' programme got him off to a poor start. If he was to complain later that he was misquoted, it was largely his fault for making himself so difficult to understand in the first instance. Experienced television performers know full well that to make demanding and intellectually stimulating remarks on the air is a risky business. In the studio the contributor might feel very much as if he is talking to friends or colleagues and can overlook the fact that what he says can be heard by thousands or millions of viewers. Challenging remarks heard by so many become controversial remarks. If care is not taken a seemingly innocent phrase can appear very different when reported by all the newspapers in cold print.

In the event, considering the normal insensitivity of the popular press to the subleties involved in reporting matter of a more obscure nature, the *Daily Mail* report of the 'Credo' programme was fair and responsible, allowing for a few detailed inaccuracies, most noticeably the paper's premature consecration of the Professor. It was the *Daily Mail* which anticipated the controversy which was to develop. The headline read: 'TURMOIL THAT HITS AT HEART OF GOING TO CHURCH':

A bishop started a major controversy yesterday by saying Jesus did not walk on water and he was not born to a virgin.

The denial of fundamental Christian teachings by the Bishop of Durham, the Rev. Professor David Jenkins, is bound to cause divisions in the Church.

And it will almost certainly lead to calls for his resignation. Appointed last month, he is the fourth highest ranking bishop in the Church of England.

He said that the walking on water story and accounts of the virginal birth were not strictly true, but were added to the story of Jesus by the early Christians to express their faith in him as the Messiah.

Many churchgoers will be upset by his view of the resurrection. During the programme, which deals with religious and moral issues, he said the resurrection was not a single event but 'a series of experiences that gradually convinced the growing number of people who became apostles that Jesus had certainly been dead, but he was raised up again, that is to say the very life and power and purpose and personality which was in him was actually continuing'.

And so it was that a university professor of theology, well-known in academic and ecumenical circles, but not to the public, soon to be elevated to the episcopacy in the ancient palatine diocese of Durham, set viewers and readers thinking. Many, who were struggling to keep a faith in the face of an onslaught of rational, scientific ideas, were encouraged and relieved to learn that a leading churchman was with them in their struggle. Others, particularly those who saw the Bible as a fundamental and divinely inspired blue-print, became worried. If the very foundations of faith were questioned or even discarded, would not the simple, trusting faith of many million souls be brutally destroyed?

4

Miracles – the twentieth-century debate

There was a time when it was accepted that just because an idea was irrational it did not mean it could not be believed. To the people of the time it would have appeared quite rational anyway. For instance it was quite rational to believe, prior to Galileo, that the sun revolved round the earth and that heavy objects fell faster than light objects when dropped from a height. Within the framework of ideas used then to interpret the world, the irrational could also be the believable.

And so it was that for many centuries the story of the virgin birth, the accounts of the gospel miracles and ultimately the biblical reports of the physical resurrection of the body of Jesus from the tomb were accepted without question.

In an age where science insists on rigorous standards of proof, such incredible reports are harder to digest. Theologians too have been caught up in the new trends; they have been seen to accept the idea that empirical evidence is the highest form of truth. Consequently they have been forced to ask themselves, do the gospel stories stand up to the sort of analysis to which they would be subjected in other disciplines? On the face of it the answer is no, or, as David Jenkins put it in a radio interview broadcast not long after the famous 'Credo' programme, 'No single historical fact can be certain . . . historical facts are a matter of probability, doubt and uncertainty . . . There is no

30

certainty in the New Testament about anything of importance.'

And yet David Jenkins and many others, both radical and middle-of-the-road theologians, are convinced within themselves that the gospel message is not a whole load of balderdash. Despite their reasoning powers they know that a spiritual dimension exists, they know of well attested modern reports of improbable deeds bordering on the miraculous, they know of such forces as love and guilt and evil.

Somehow a coherence has to be found. Two seemingly contradictory forces have to be reconciled and that reconciliation, they say, can be achieved not by reading the Bible and accepting it at face value, but by delving into the Bible's history and language and sorting the poetry from the allegory, the parables from the history, the reflection from the polemic.

Scholars have a number of techniques at their disposal. First of all there is a simple comparison of one gospel account of an event with the account of the same event in a different Gospel. The details included or excluded are tell-tale signs when it comes to sorting out who wrote the Gospels and why. The Easter morning story in St Mark's Gospel, for instance, gives no hint that the women who arrived in the garden at dawn to find an empty tomb were witnessing anything supernatural. St Matthew, however, talks of a violent earthquake and an angel with 'face like lightning, his garments were white as snow' rolling away the stone.

Secondly, the Gospels and other books can be studied for clues as to when they were written. If, for instance, it can be argued that Matthew's Gospel was written after Mark's it could be argued that the supernatural detail was a later addition to the resurrection narrative. And if that was the case the question must be asked, why was it added. Was it because the Gospels were written for different readerships?

31

Thirdly, the Gospels can now be compared with the other religious writings of the early Church. There were more than four gospels written and it was not until the fourth century A.D. that the Bible in its familiar form took shape.

Fourthly, there is the study of language, both to assist in the dating of the Bible and also to verify that no meanings were lost in translation. The word 'virgin' for instance, used in the Gospels to describe Mary and quoted from the prophecy of Isaiah that a 'virgin shall conceive' could be a misinterpretation, and really be a reference to a young woman.

Fifthly, there is a study of culture. Were some parts of the New Testament specially written for the Jews as opposed to the Gentiles? What influence did Roman and Greek thought have on the writers?

Sixthly, the gospel accounts can be checked against historical evidence from other sources. Pontius Pilate, for example, crops up in Roman histories of the period. His name also appears on an inscription found in the ruins of a temple at Caesarea.

The use of such techniques is not an exact science. There are many basic areas of disagreement, especially concerning the dating of the books of the New Testament. On one point most scholars however agree. The Gospels were not written by Matthew, Mark, Luke and John as straightforward eye-witness accounts of what happened during the years of Christ's ministry on earth. Which Gospel came first is still very much open to debate.

One of the biggest divides between the experts concerns the way the evidence of the Bible texts should be used. Some see the Bible as an important collection of raw historical data to be considered alongside other documents of similar antiquity and treated with scepticism and ruthless thoroughness. Others say the Bible should be treated differently and reverently as the inspired word of God written albeit by the hand of man, but with the guidance of the Holy Spirit and confirmed by centuries of tradition.

But even those scholars who apply rigorous standards of examination to the gospel stories know they cannot dismiss the essential meaning behind the stories. If at first sight the stories fail to stand up as history, then, they reason, the stories must have another purpose. If the story of a body rising from the dead seems improbable to the scholar, and yet that same searching scholar feels in his heart of hearts the living spirit of that man crucified, there has to be some explanation for the story. The feeling is real enough and cannot be denied.

There are some theologians who don't feel the spirit of God in themselves but know from other evidence that the spirit of God must exist. They too can explore the Gospels knowing that in them, even if historical evidence is lacking, there is a deep mystery, a riddle to be solved.

David Jenkins has explored both avenues to an understanding of God, both direct personal experience and the use of exterior reasoning.

He talks of times when he was in Beirut for the World Council of Churches and walking and talking with an Orthodox colleague, and how he experienced a third unseen presence as they walked, giving a special almost mystical meaning to their deliberations. He also is happy to adopt the analogies of physics to describe God. 'It is as if you're trying to prove the existence of particles which you can't touch and can't see and which only exist for the briefest of moments. You have evidence of their existence only by tracking where they have been and what they have been doing.'

In the nineteenth century, Charles Darwin's *Origin of Species* questioned the accepted wisdom of the age. The scientific community accepted his ideas as a coherent way of explaining the existence of the fossil records. Although the Darwinian theory has been modified by subsequent generations, there are few people today who still hold fast

33

to the Genesis account of creation as an historical record. In the popular mind the biblical tale of a world created in six days has been entirely replaced by a rather over-simplified set of Darwinian notions. There are certainly today very few leading churchmen who accept the creation story as told, and to take a more scientific view of the origins of the world, they say, in no way undermines their faith.

The twentieth-century equivalent to the creation debate has been that involving the miracles. The literal meaning of parts of the Bible which have appeared 'unscientific' has been reinterpreted to fit in with current fashions of thought. There are therefore twentieth-century theologians who argue that a belief in the virgin birth or the supernatural resurrection of the body of Jesus is not an essential foundation of the Christian faith. This approach however has not been widely known about. It has tended to stay cloistered in academic circles. It has not been in general circulation. Most lay people and churchgoers have until very recently been in no doubt that a belief in miracles was part and parcel of faith. Those who could not accept the miracles assumed therefore that they had no faith. Some, being unable to deny a spiritual dimension to life, looked for explanations in religions and practices other than Christianity. The debate triggered off by David Jenkins' 'Credo' interview has, while alarming many of the faithful, given hope to many who feared they were without faith.

5

An ancient heresy revived?

There are those, particularly on the evangelical wing of the Church, who argue that what the liberal theologians are saying is not new, has nothing to do with the dawn of the Age of Reason and is but a reiteration of heresies almost as old as Christianity itself. What is new, they say, is that these 'heresies' have become so prevalent and respectable amongst the intelligentsia of the Church. It is almost as if 'modern-thinking' church leaders take an elitist attitude to theology, they claim, indulging in semantic and obscure arguments amongst themselves while preaching a simple faith to those in the pews, believing the ordinary worshipper to be unable to digest anything too complicated and demanding. At best the 'elite' is accused of hypocrisy, at worst, deceit. While such strong accusations are denied, many modern theologians do accept that between the theorist and the worshipper a gap of incomprehension is too often discernible.

One academic in the forefront of the debate is Professor Keith Ward of King's College, London. He was quoted in the 'Credo' programme but gave, as a theologian, a more substantial interview in the BBC Radio 4 programme 'Soundings' transmitted a few weeks later. He confirmed the fears of the evangelicals that David Jenkins' views would not be out of place on the Bench of Bishops, and then explained how it would be possible for someone to believe in the resurrection without believing in the literal raising of a crucified body from the dead:

'I believe in the resurrection in what I take to be an absolutely orthodox sense. And that sense is given in 1 Corinthians 15, that the resurrection of the body is a spiritual body and not a body of flesh and blood, which Paul says cannot inherit the Kingdom. So when you ask about a resurrection there is a tendency for later mythology to come into this, and people think of it as the body getting out of the tomb and walking away. That's not the account in the Bible. So, if you want to be truthful to the Bible, you've got to say the body did not get up and walk away – it disappeared, totally, and what appeared to the apostles was a different sort of manifestation or appearance altogether, a spiritual and glorified body. Now clearly that is not the sort of thing which would be a corpse walking around.'

There are even those modern theologians who would argue that if archaeologists were to unearth a body in Jerusalem and prove it to be that of Jesus, it would make relatively little difference to their faith. What matters, they say, is a Christian's having an awareness of the living presence of Christ. Not that that idea finds much favour in the evangelical camp. The notion was described by Dr Richard France, Head of the Department of Biblical Studies at the London Bible College, as theologically defective:

'It seems to me the Christian faith must be based on what Jesus actually did rather than on a sort of disembodied belief which occurred at some time later. This view seems to me to divorce Christianity from Jesus in a way I find quite unacceptable. But also, and I think this is most important, historically I would find it unacceptable, because I do not find it possible to study the Gospels as if the writers didn't care about the factuality of what they wrote. This doesn't seem to me to ring true. It's very true to modern existentialist thought but it's not true, as far as I understand, to first-century Jewish thought. And if

36

somebody in first-century Palestine said Jesus is risen from the dead that meant there is no body in the tomb; and therefore either the evangelists are not telling the truth or we have got to take very seriously the historical factuality of the resurrection. Granted of course there are many problems, many inconsistencies between the accounts of the resurrection; that I am perfectly prepared to grant, and I don't think it's possible to achieve a total harmonization of all that's in the accounts. The stories have come to us through a process of transmission in the Church which allowed for a great deal of flexibility in the way in which they were told. Probably, and this is still a matter for considerable debate, there would have been about a generation during which the stories were retold, often orally, possibly being written down within ten or twenty years. But this is very speculative, and obviously the details are going to vary in that process. That doesn't worry me at all. What would worry me is the suggestion that in the course of that very short period, while eye-witnesses were still alive, one could simply invent a physical resurrection which had never happened.'

Interestingly, the gap between Dr France and Professor Ward is not very wide. They are far closer than the supposed existence of a controversy between the conservatives and the 'moderns' would suggest. Professor Ward accepts the tomb was empty and that the apostles witnessed a manifestation. Dr France acknowledges the problems of detailed gospel story inconsistencies and uses explanations of a type more associated with the liberals to explain them. Professor Ward is well aware of the way Bible stories can become embellished with time, and he points to the Christmas story as an example. Nowhere, for instance, does Matthew's Gospel say of the 'Three Kings' that either there were three or that they were kings.

'The story itself is much more reserved,' says Professor

Ward. 'You probably have to think of a group of rather scruffy astrologers coming over from the eastern parts of Syria. And to accept even that as historical I have to admit that the evidence is not good. Any Christian has the right to say, I don't know if it happened or not.

'The most interesting question is why was the story written into the text? Why were the Gospels written? They were not written as history, they were talking of events which had happened eighty years previously. I don't for a moment believe all the sayings and happenings were remembered word for word and then miraculously written down. The Gospels were written to bring out the immense spiritual significance of a risen Christ. That is, that God was now known through the person of Jesus Christ, as a living presence within the Church. The Gospel writers were using historical traditions but using them very freely. In Judaism there's a tradition, "*haggadah*", by which you use stories and tell them with all sorts of elaborations and exaggerations to make a symbolic point. And this is an accepted tradition. It's not a matter of telling lies, but it's not a matter of just telling the plain truth either. It's "faction". You tell a story which has a historical basis, but you elaborate and you put in details, and those details are put in to make a specific point. The story of the three wise men might have been written to make the point that Jesus was a revelation to the Gentiles and as a recognition of Christ's messiahship. There were very good symbolic points there. I would have thought it was based on some historic tradition, but exactly what it was is, to be honest, quite irrecoverable. We simply cannot know what the fact was behind the fiction.'

Dr France says that his students from the evangelical tradition cannot isolate themselves from modern biblical criticism. They must brace themselves for any challenges.

'Criticism as such is neutral,' he says, 'It's critics who are not. Critical study of the Bible means studying the Bible with all the resources available and all the acumen we can bring to it, doing our best to make sense of it within its own historical and theological context. But how you do that depends entirely on the presuppositions with which you come to it.

'No historian has ever written a book without an axe to grind and without a point to put across. No history is purely objective. And the fact that the Gospels are in a sense propaganda, they have a message to get across, does not suggest to me that they are therefore unhistorical. And if a person tells a story which gets across a theological point, my first question is not, is it therefore untrue? but, how has he angled the story in the telling of it so as to get across the theology and what does this tell me about what the actual event was which he is recording? That's where the creativity of the Christian writer seems to me to come in. Not at the level of inventing things out of whole cloth – because I cannot see that that is something for which there is any evidence in the New Testament, or, as far as I can tell, in Jewish recording of recent history in the first century A.D. While in their embellishment of ancient history, from the Old Testament period, Jewish writers were prepared to add factors which had no basis in the Old Testament record, when it comes to the recording of recent history I see very little evidence for simple invention.'

To the average person struggling with the problems of daily life the arguments of New Testament scholars often seem peripheral and self-indulgent. Following the 'Credo' programme, the Bishop of Durham recounts, with some satisfaction, that he had overheard a theological debate between two shoppers in a cake shop. Prior to the Bishop of Durham affair's taking to the airwaves however, the issues which roused such passion in academic circles were rarely aired in Church. Indeed, as one distinguished academic, Miss Ruth Etchells, Principal of St John's

College, Durham, put it on the Radio 4 programme 'Soundings', churchgoers are people who do not, by and large, ask questions. They receive the Scriptures as a form of assurance of the basis of their worship.

'Academic theologians exist however to push out the boundaries of understanding. Sometimes, the questioning scholar, who is also a churchgoer is in disjunction. All too often there is a gulf of understanding between those in academic circles and those in church on Sunday.

'It is a frightening gap. People like me who are working in the theological colleges have an absolute obligation to help those who are going to be the leaders of the churches, the parish priests, the deaconnesses, to help them to be 'bridge' people; because on the one hand their feet are firmly planted in the worshipping community, that is their weekly life, that is their charge, their cure of souls; and yet on the other hand they have undergone in that seminar room, that experience, that excitement of working at the detailed speculation about how Scripture has been formed. And therefore they are in a position to assist the worshipping community to perceive what it is that the academic theologians are doing and how it can enrich their believing life. Where the difference of task has not been perceived, so that what the academic theologians say seems directly to attack the authority of the book under which we sit, then there is a real desire to protect that worshipping community from what might destroy it.

'That's on the one hand: on the other there is a genuine difficulty in finding a bridging language – because we're talking about the language of praise which has to grow from the full experience of the believer's life, part of which is growing – and that means probing and pressing and looking at the difficulties – and part of which is affirming, which is the exact opposite. Finding a language sensitive to both those activities to be used by people whose life

40

has not been the seminar room, is a very tricky problem indeed.'

To what extent, one could ask, is it honest for an academic theologian to go to Church at all? Especially if in doing so he or she suspends his or her critical faculties and joins in with the general unquestioning affirmation of faith. Ruth Etchells answers the question in this way:

'I would have thought that the academic was not suspending his or her critical faculties; what was happening was a recognition that at this point I am suspending questions of the day time, which is my job, in order to express my affirmation in the God I believe in. And if I didn't keep on doing that I might find myself navel-gazing, in that I would be intrigued by the intellectual questions rather than the God I was pursuing. So it is essential that that affirmation goes on.'

How far should the academic push the boundaries of questioning? Is there a point at which the day-time academic suddenly thinks, perhaps there is nothing?

'This has happened in some cases. And the accusation that one or two people have made, that there are some academic theologians who have so emptied the faith of content that there is nothing left to defend, that's a genuine accusation. But it is not a logical consequence of questioning. There are a variety of tasks. What one must be prepared to do in all honesty is to face the dangerous consequences of one's task. That's a matter of intellectual honesty. But one does it because one starts from an absolute commitment, not just to God, but to God in Jesus Christ. And I think at the end of the day one has to recognize also that the human intellect is limited and is more limited than the human spirit. Reason is an inadequate tool. Reason must be used to one's absolute limit because it is God-given, but if it is

41

seen as the ultimate way of perceiving God and understanding theological proposition then it will fail – just as if one reads poetry with reason only, one fails. And one of the dangers, it seems to me, in contemporary argument is the pinning of the entire argument on the rational. If you are dealing in religion you are also dealing in mystery, and recognition of the mystery is all important. I would have thought recognizing that mystery is the rational thing to do.'

Knowing when one has reached the limit of one's reasoning powers is not easy. 'To begin with,' Bishop Jenkins says, 'in the reasoning process one is using logic to create order from a muddle. But one has to know where muddle is not, in fact, disorder but mystery.'

The new theological student can find the cold dismembering of his faith a disturbing experience, particularly if he has come to a college possessing a simple, uncluttered enthusiasm. He might not fully realize that the purpose behind the dismembering of faith is to reconstruct it, but the process can be painful. That process is then followed by a series of difficult decisions as to how much of that painful process should be shared with the congregation he then has in his charge.

At the height of the Durham affair a group of five ordinands, from Queen's College, Birmingham, amongst them both Anglicans and Methodists, were invited to reflect on some of these problems on BBC Radio. Did investigation harm faith?, they were asked.

'No, it doesn't, it opens up the whole Bible to faith, in some instances. But we also have to let the Bible speak to us, as well as applying our critical minds to it.'

'I think one has to ground one's faith in the fact that God is able to speak directly to man and that the essential way this was done was through the life of Jesus of Nazareth. So to that extent I would argue an historical Jesus and an historical crucifixion are essential. As to the resurrection, I personally wouldn't need that, in the sense of an empty tomb and the events as described in the added postscripts of the four Gospels.

'But anybody who got up in the pulpit on their first Easter Sunday in a parish and said you didn't have to believe in the gospel accounts of the resurrection, would be a fool. That would be destructive. In a sense we are trying to convey to our congregation the results of a couple of hundred years of serious scholarship and thought about the New Testament – so one can't be bald-headed and say that to a congregation in a parish.'

'As for the Christmas story, the inner meaning is a very radical one. God chose to send his son in such a way as to show us he identifies himself with those who are the poorest and those for whom society has least use. I don't accept the angels and the three wise men and so on literally, but I don't need to worry about the literal meaning in that there are many things which are written which don't have necessarily a literal meaning but nevertheless contain the profoundest truth.

'In no sense is the Bible becoming less important. It remains absolutely central to Christian faith, but it has to be used in perhaps a different way to the way in which it was a couple of centuries ago.'

'Too often we can underestimate the abilities of our congregation and must be prepared to bring the debate to them. We think they need more spoon-feeding than they actually do. There are people who really do want to think and if you are in your circuit or parish and want to organize some classes to really look at the Bible, then you can introduce ideas in such a way that says there are going to be challenges, there are going to be issues to be faced and you introduce them in such a way that people know to what they are coming.'

'I am not going to duck these issues but am quite sure the pulpit is not the right place from which to introduce them. The parson's study, the Bible-study group, the fellowship group, the joining together and searching of Christian minds and hearts, that is the place to do it. It is a time for great tolerance and for searching together; whatever our differences we must accept in faith that we are being moved by the spirit.'

'In a strange way the Bible seems to sort us out – whether we are fundamentalists or more critical.'

Biblical criticism is to be found too in Roman Catholic seminaries, though within the Catholic Church ideas developing from the latest investigation into the real meaning behind the Scriptures, have received less prominence; at least in that there is no British Catholic controversialist akin to Bishop Jenkins. In the parishes amongst younger priests, however, the new ideas can be found. Father Keith Barltrop is an assistant priest in a north London suburban parish and is well aware of the problems of transporting the ideas of the seminar room into the parish situation.

'The working mother who is bringing her three young children along to Mass is concerned about other things, as are electricians, teachers or lorry drivers. Indeed they can be quite shocked and I have on occasion had to pick up the pieces after people have accidentally heard some of the new notions. I get them to say why it disturbs them and I get them, hopefully, to adopt a more intelligent attitude to the Bible than the rather simple, uncritical one they have had. What we as priests and lay leaders are trying to do is trying to awaken that simple faith, not so much by indulging in

44

biblical criticism but by somehow giving them a living experience as to what their faith really means. Trying to make it come alive. Once they've got that they can then cope with all the critical questions. But if they haven't, if they've just got that very simple faith which Granny or Mummy and Daddy handed down, then naturally it is going to be a bit of a shock.

'It is the difference between telling the truth and telling the whole truth. Nobody really tells the whole truth to everybody all the time. On the other hand we do have a duty to lead people into the whole truth. After all that is what Jesus himself said he came to do. But first of all we have to waken the faith and give them some experience of the living community of faith – of people in small groups who share a faith you can almost touch and see. When you have got that, you can then begin to say the Bible doesn't literally have to be true in all its historic details. Their faith is then grounded in something else. I am a priest, a pastor, and my ultimate concern is to care for people and that involves challenging them and at times protecting them. One must of course do both; protection without challenge is as bad as challenge without protection. One has got to get a balance there.'

Dr France also points out that a sermon can benefit from, and be given new authority by, a lot of behind-the-scenes critical study without the congregation having to be aware of the details of that study.

'It is rather like what they used to say in examination books – rough work must be presented with the answer. I don't believe that when it comes to preaching. The rough work is done in the study, it doesn't have to be presented with the answer in the pulpit. I would not share my uncertainties with a congregation unless I was pretty clear that this was something which needed to be shared with them.

'I would not preach a certainty, having at the back of

my mind an uncertainty. I think I would preach in such a way that the uncertainty I still had to resolve was not played off on the congregation until I had resolved it. If I got to the point of believing an historical resurrection to be unnecessary, then I would have a duty to preach that, but all of that is purely hypothetical because I do believe the historic resurrection is vital and the more I study it the more I come to that conclusion.'

'The Bible is the inspired word of God,' Professor Ward says unhesitatingly. 'But what was God trying to say? Was he trying to give the facts about history or give the meaning of Jesus' life, presented through a series of stories based on historical recollection? I think the latter. It is a terrible mistake made by people, usually with a scientific background to think the Bible is science. It tells you the facts which you just have to learn; it's not particularly religion, just a lot of history. It's essential, it seems to me, to get this sense of a story with a spiritual meaning and to say, if you ask me what actually happened, as a historian I can't tell you, though I believe there was a historical basis to it. There was a Jesus, there were wonderful things happening, he did heal people; but did this happen or that happen precisely? Honesty requires you to say, I don't know exactly what happened. What we have are the later accounts of the deeds, meant to convey a spiritual meaning.'

To what extent however are theologians like Keith Ward putting themselves through all sorts of verbal hoops to justify to themselves a faith in which they now only half believe?

'People have forgotten what religious stories are all about, namely, they are about the mystery of God which is symbolized in myths and stories and they are not about straightforward things you can take with a cine camera or record;

46

so that is what has gone wrong. It's not that theologians are suffering from half belief. They are trying to escape from that terrible perversion of religion where it's interpreted as science. Religion's not about that, it's about your soul's eternal relationship with God. Theologians say, Look at the Gospel records in the light of what they tell you of your relationship with God.'

In the debate brought out into the open by the Bishop of Durham there is this curious paradox. The modern theologians who are accused of allowing the scientific age to dominate their understanding of the Bible in turn accuse the conservatives of being too 'scientific' in their study of the Scriptures.

6

'A dangerous and foolish heresy'

On 30 April 1984, the day after the 'Credo' broadcast, two pupils at the Hereford Cathedral School showed their chaplain, the Reverend William Ledwich, the report in the *Daily Mail* of the interview with the Bishop-designate of Durham. This edition of the paper carried the headline 'THE FAKE MIRACLES OF JESUS, BY A BISHOP'. Alarmed by what he saw, William Ledwich called the Church Information Office in Westminster. They confirmed a date for David Jenkins' consecration had been set for 6 July. Feeling there was little time to lose, William Ledwich drew up a petition asking the Archbishop of York to think again about consecrating the new bishop.

Although William Ledwich was to become one of the most active opponents of the appointment, he was not alone. The Reverend Tony Higton, founder of the pressure group Action for Biblical Witness to our Nation, undertook a massive mailing to sound out the opinions of the clergy at large. The Evangelical and Anglo-Catholic wings of the Church had found a common cause. The issue was raised at diocesan level in Durham and elsewhere, with a third group of opponents also emerging – those who thought that, while misguided views could be tolerated coming from academics, bishops-designate were expected to exercise greater self-control. The *Church Times* reflected this approach in its editorial, having noted that the volume of mostly hostile correspondence it had received on the subject was larger than it had known for many years.

One lesson to be learned from this affair is that even the prospect of a mitre makes a man news – and therefore makes it essential that he should weigh his utterances, particularly on TV, knowing that they may well reach a public not in a position to appreciate learned nuances of thought. Another lesson is that theology is too important to be left to academic theologians. Many bishops, priests and laypeople are called to think deeply and to teach clearly about the great truths of the gospel in response to the age's basic and outspoken questions.

The following week a letter from David Jenkins, was published thanking the *Church Times* for its careful and courteous editorial. He had this to say to his critics:

Apostolic and missionary responsibility for the Christian faith demands, not the defence of credal formulae, but the exploration and exposition of the great Catholic symbols in the light of the best current knowledge and the deepest contemporary experience. The future of the Church lies with God's liveliness, not with our defensiveness.

Nearly fifty years of conscious Christian discipleship and well over thirty years of passionate study and teaching at all levels and in many places have convinced me that facing the issues of critical study, historical knowledge and scientific thinking are essential to mission to our unbelieving and would-be believing fellows, as well as to the freedom and growth of our own Christian souls. As I approach my new apostolate I therefore naturally and obediently take every opportunity for facing, and insist that others face, these demands and opportunities. I shall continue to do so.

The evidence that I shall take the promises required of a bishop in good faith and in humble obedience can be found as to the past in my writings and from those who have heard me. The evidence as to the future will be found, by God's grace, in the collaborative teaching and serving which I shall work at within my diocese and elsewhere.

Now, as always, I remain dependent for the authenticity of my ministry and the correction of the numerous faults which I personally and repeatedly bring to it on the prayers and support of my friends and fellow disciples, and on the grace and forgiveness of God the Holy Trinity.

Nevertheless the campaign to persuade the Archbishop of York to defer the service of consecration was gathering momentum. It was fuelled by an editorial in the evangelical *Church of England Newspaper* which was quite different in tone from that in the *Church Times*:

If a man who takes pride in peddling dangerous and foolish heresy can become a senior leader of the Church, we have forfeited the right to be called a Christian denomination. . . .

[The Professor] is not a Christian believer in the New Testament sense; he is a hindrance rather than a help to the people of God; he should not be allowed to take up his appointment.

By the beginning of June the Reverend Tony Higton had committed £2,000 to his mail campaign. In the coming weeks every ordained Anglican clergyman in England was to receive a letter and a 'freepost' reply slip asking for support for the statement, 'I strongly disapprove of Professor Jenkins' recent statements as Bishop-elect of Durham.' Mr Higton's parish, Hawkwell in Essex, became the headquarters of a new organization, Action for Biblical Witness to Our Nation (ANWON) which set out its aims as 'to do something positive about the theological and moral confusions in the Church of England; the failure of the

50

Church to evangelize to the nation; the need for the Holy Spirit to renew the life of the Church'.

Meanwhile William Ledwich's petition was collecting signatures rapidly. On the Radio 4 programme 'Sunday' at the end of May, David Jenkins was asked about his reaction to the growing opposition to his consecration: 'I must admit, it hurts more than I expected. What I particularly find hurtful is that people think I am some cold, detached, academic, questioning person. . . . Actually I am a very warm, committed, questioning person.'

Listening to that same edition of 'Sunday', tuned in for news of the Billy Graham Rally, was the Reverend David Holloway, the vicar of Jesmond, Newcastle. What he heard from the Bishop-designate prompted him into action. Amongst David Jenkins' remarks was this one: 'Supposing the tomb was empty, and it may have been, that is not the resurrection. The resurrection is being sure of the Living Lord.' – the implication being that as an historical event the resurrection was a possibility but not a certainty.

The 'Sunday' programme mentioned the petition which was by then gathering momentum. David Holloway thought more formal action should be taken and formed the view that David Jenkins should publicly affirm that he believed the Gospel as taught by the Church of England. First, however, he wrote to *The Times*. He argued that since historians can be certain of their facts, Dr Jenkins' scepticism about this 'is sheer nonsense'. And he asked, 'Is it right that David Jenkins should allow himself to go forward for consecration? We can't have bishops whose teaching undermines the truth of the resurrection.'

Next, David Holloway convened a meeting of eleven proctors of the Convocation of York (clerical members of Synod). They wrote to the Archbishop of York; the letter was sent on 22 June.

Recent public statements of the Professor regarding history, the New Testament, the Virgin Birth and, especially the Resurrection of Jesus Christ have deeply distressed many Church members and caused considerable public controversy and disquiet. In these circumstances we believe that the General Synod itself should be able to hear, publicly, your statement and to ask its own 'Questions' *before* the Consecration takes place. When there is so much disquiet it would be unfortunate for the Consecration to take place the very day before the Synod assembles as is planned at present.

Canon C18 1 ('Every bishop is . . . to uphold sound and wholesome doctrine, and to banish and drive away all erroneous and strange opinions; and . . . to set forward and maintain quietness, love, and peace among all men') morally, if not legally, seems to us to require that the Consecration does not take place until certain issues are discussed and clarified.

We genuinely wish to isolate these issues from the 'person' of Professor Jenkins, whom we admire for his honesty and openness. We believe that good will come from wise but frank and free discussion. The issues cannot be ignored.

On Monday, 11 June, the Dean and Chapter of Durham Cathedral met after Evensong to elect a new bishop. They met in private to consider the one name presented to them by the Queen. Until recently a Chapter which failed to elect the Queen's nominee was 'subject to the severest penalties'. That no longer applies and indeed the meeting of the Durham Chapter to elect a bishop in the old way was one of the last gatherings of its kind. (The new Appointment of Bishops Measure, which in June 1984 was awaiting parliamentary approval, makes such elections unnecessary.) Following the meeting in the chapter house, the Dean, the six residentiary canons and twenty-four honorary canons issued a statement confirming David Jenkins' election and assuring him of a welcome to the diocese. The Dean, the Very Reverend Peter Baelz, said,

'I am delighted he is to be our Bishop. He has so much to give us, even though it looks at times as if it might be a slightly rough ride.'

The only hope left now for the opponents to his consecration was for the Archbishop of York to intervene. The Archbishop was to receive no shortage of advice. Not only were the Evangelicals and the Anglo-Catholics going for David Jenkins; a body of opinion was forming which held that, whatever the validity of his views, it would be in the best interests of all that he step down, because he had raised such a storm and was such a divisive influence in the Church. An editorial in The *Daily Telegraph* of 30 May reflected that opinion. It said of the Bishop-elect's views that they were

> profoundly destructive of the peace and unity which it is a bishop's particular duty to foster, and that what the ordinary man in the pew increasingly expects from his bishop is a clear assertion of the living Christian tradition he has received. Professor Jenkins must now face an unenviable choice. Either to withdraw and return to academic life or to press on in the knowledge that his election would be pastorally deeply divisive. Many would say that, though painful, withdrawal is the wiser choice.

Far from making any attempt to dampen down the row it had sparked off, the 'Credo' programme, on 24 June added further fuel to the flames. It broadcast a poll of bishops and claimed that a significant number of diocesan bishops shared David Jenkins' reservations about the traditional view of the Gospel miracles. A number of bishops later claimed they had been polled unfairly or in a meaningless way; the Bishop of Chester, for instance, was telephoned at five past six after a hectic day just as he was trying to snatch a quick meal before leaving for a confirmation service.

'If I had refused to answer, that would have been one less bishop; but I found that her approach was a talking-round-things rather than any direct questions – apart from, "Are you prepared to be quoted?" Although I am sure that the interviewers would have done their best to present what they believed to be the assembled ideas, I have little faith that they are really accurate about the opinions of bishops.

'Questions were so wrapped up that it was difficult to know how to answer in some matters. If they had asked directly, "Do you believe in the virgin birth and do you believe in the resurrection of Jesus Christ?" then there could have been an assembly of facts rather than an assembly of estimates.,

However unscientific the poll might have been it neverthe-less served to confirm the suspicions of many traditionalists that heresies were rife in the highest places in the Church. As did the response of the Archbishop of York whose stand, or lack of it, was such as to put him firmly in the sights of those gunning for David Jenkins.

On the afternoon of Sunday, 1 July, William Ledwich, a small party from Hereford and two priests (one Evan-gelical, one Anglo-Catholic) from York Diocese went to Bishopthorpe, the Archbishop's home. They carried with them a copy of Mr Ledwich's petition signed by twelve-and-a-half-thousand communicants.

The Archbishop accepted the thick bundle of papers. Later that evening he received a fifteen-strong delegation from Durham convened by the Reverend Ian Palmer, Vicar of Annfield Plain near Stanley. Following the meeting Mr Palmer admitted he had gone with hope but 'left without it . . . We asked that David Jenkins make a public and positive affirmation of the cardinal truths prior to the conse-cration. We were told that this was not possible.'

Of the day's meetings, Mr Ledwich said, 'The Arch-bishop listened with a closed mind. His decision had been made, the consecration would go ahead.'

Three days later, and only two days before the service in York Minster at which David Jenkins would become a bishop, the Archbishop published a detailed reply to the petitioners. He carefully avoided giving his own view on the issues involved, saying that his role as Archbishop was 'to keep the ring, as it were in the Church of England and define the limits within which one can believe'.

During the consecration service, the Archbishop said, he would be asking David Jenkins specifically if he believed the doctrine of the Christian faith as the Church of England has received it.

'From what I know of him personally and from his writings, I have every reason to believe that he will be able to answer this question affirmatively and in complete good faith.

'Apart from the recitation of the Nicene Creed during the Eucharist, these are the only explicit forms of doctrinal assent which the liturgy requires, and I see no valid grounds for asking Professor Jenkins to make more declarations than the Church has seen fit to prescribe.'

The Archbishop of York did however air one note of reservation in his support for David Jenkins. It can be argued, he wrote, that he has been

unwise in the manner he has expressed himself publicly. No doubt he will quickly learn that the way a bishop is heard differs from the way a professor is heard, and that the impression conveyed through the media may be more significant than what is actually said or left unsaid. In any attempt to communicate profound truths, public relations cannot be ignored. Nevertheless, it would be a strange reflection on the Church's integrity if in so important a matter as the choice of a man to be bishop, it were to pay more attention to the image than to the reality.

It is a frequently used ploy, commonly found when individuals, usually holders of high office, or institutions feel they have been misunderstood, that they blame the media. It is true the media deal in snippets and quotes and images and have little understanding of nuances. But the snippets and quotes selected by the hardened hacks of Fleet Street and the 'trendy' television producers are normally those which represent the broad meaning of what the speaker is trying to say. Issues can be trivialized or over-personalized, but the experienced headline writer normally gets to the heart of the matter with unswerving precision. When speakers complain, it is often not because they have been misquoted, although that is what they say, but because they have been quoted all too accurately and their heart exposed. When David Jenkins was quoted, a debate at the very heart of the Church was exposed and the leadership was embarrassed – especially in that some of the more enthusiastic members of the Church, on the high and low wings, were, for the first time, learning that the debate was not just confined to a few dons but had penetrated the Church to a degree they had not previously appreciated.

In William Ledwich's case that realization had taken place slowly over nine years. The David Jenkins business was, so to speak, the last straw. He wrote as follows in his book *The Durham Affair*.

I was very conscious that the Durham affair was not an isolated outburst by an eccentric academic, but the symptoms of a deep sickness in the Church of England . .
I was becoming increasingly disturbed by the growth of what I shall call 'liberalism' in the Church. Many priests were denying very fundamental doctrines of the faith. Dr Jenkins was no extremist, no exception. He was a typical moderate. Others, many others, expressed the view that not only the Virgin Birth and the Empty Tomb, but also the Incarnation itself was a myth . . .
There was Don Cupitt, whose book *Taking Leave of God*

56

clearly showed that whatever he meant by the word 'god', he did not believe in the God who had revealed himself as the Father of Jesus Christ. As his recent television series shows, he is nearer Buddhism than Christianity. Yet he and many of the contributors to *The Myth of God Incarnate* are still practising and licenced Anglican clergy. I have met and heard many such Anglican clergy since my ordination whose views vary from classical Arian or gnostic heresies to virtual atheism. All this seemed to be justified on the theory of comprehensiveness, the alleged glory of Anglicanism. But I could not make sense of such a theory. Certainly the Church may allow disagreement on matters of uncertain opinions, but can she do so on matters of revealed doctrine? It was denied that fundamental doctrine was at stake, but I was unconvinced.

7

The roots of the debate

'I am compelled, under an overwhelming sense of responsibility, to address to you a solemn protest . . . His expressed beliefs touching the fundamental matters of faith seem to me incompatible with the sincere profession of the Creeds . . . His treatment of the Virgin Birth seems incompatible with personal belief in its occurrence . . . He repudiates any insistence upon the "empty tomb" and declares it to have no significance.'

These words of the Bishop of Oxford were uttered, not as might be supposed in 1984 with references to David Jenkins, but in 1917. The man under attack was Dr Hensley Henson, then nominated as Bishop of Hereford, later, by coincidence, to become Bishop of Durham.

The then Bishop of Oxford's words were quoted in *The Times* on 5 July 1984. In a leader devoted to the imminent consecration of David Jenkins, *The Times* made a point of the fact that while at the time of his appointment to the See of Hereford, Dr Henson was feared by many to be an unsuitable modern, today he is remembered as 'a quintessential Anglican, an ornament of the Church, and on the testimony of his contemporaries, an excellent diocesan bishop'.

Of the Durham affair, *The Times* went on to say, 'What we are witnessing is an irregular fixture in the Anglican Calendar which has been played every twenty years or so since 1860, when the publication of *Essays and Reviews* marked the welcome or unwelcome fact that the Church of England had taken modernism into its system.'

On two occasions at least the Church made a formal attempt to address itself to the issue of 'modernism' and provide guidance to the faithful. In his reply to William Ledwich's petition the Archbishop of York made specific reference to the reports of the Doctrine Commission of 1938 and 1981.

The 1938 Report on Doctrine recognized that the Creeds contain many types of statement in which the borderline between the symbolic and the historical dimensions cannot be precisely defined, and it explicitly affirmed a liberty of interpretation. It was careful, however, to stress that such liberty must not be taken so far as to undermine the historical basis of the Gospel itself. In its own words: 'It is essential to hold that the facts underlying the gospel story – which story the Creeds summarise and interpret – were such as to justify the gospel itself.' To this extent the 1938 Report provides backing for the statement in the notes to the petition that 'we are not at liberty to reinterpret the Scriptures and Creeds in a way which denies their content'. But, unlike the petition, the Report did not conclude from this affirmation of the historical basis of Christianity, that everything stated in a historical form must necessarily be interpreted as literal history.

The 1981 Doctrine Report, *Believing in the Church*, assumed a similar liberty of interpretation, and its use of the word 'story' to describe the content of Christian tradition deliberately kept open the same options which the 1938 Commission had been at pains to safeguard.

The two reports were 'received' by the Church and had been prepared by distinguished churchmen, the 1938 report being produced under the chairmanship of William Temple, but they never became 'official party policy'.

Where however does a 'liberty of interpretation' become

licence? There would probably be some measure of agreement between liberals and conservatives on an answer to that question. The liberty exists to interpret the creeds and the Scriptures in order to determine the original meaning. The theologian must always ask, How accurately do the Gospel stories as we know them, and the creeds as we recite them, and the traditions of the Church as they have been handed down, reflect the true meaning behind the sayings and deeds of Jesus? Interpretation therefore is detective work: taking the Bible and the creeds and tracing them back to their origins rather than extrapolating from them. So it is that an understanding of how the creeds in their present form came to be established as the standard recitation of belief is important, along with an appreciation of how the books of the New Testament in their familiar form came to be chosen.

The Protestant, Eastern Orthodox and Roman Catholic Churches all share the same basic profession of faith, the creed drawn up in Constantinople in 381 and called the Nicene creed. The following is the Book of Common Prayer Version.

I believe in one God the Father Almighty, Maker of heaven and earth, And of all things visible and invisible:

And in one Lord Jesus Christ, the only-begotten Son of God, Begotten of his Father before all worlds, God of God, Light of Light, Very God of Very God, Begotten, not made, Being of one substance with the Father; By whom all things were made: Who for us men, and for our salvation, came down from heaven, And was incarnate by the Holy Ghost of the Virgin Mary, And was made man, And was crucified also for us under Pontius Pilate. He suffered and was buried, And the third day he rose again according to the Scriptures, And ascended into heaven, And sitteth on the right hand of the Father. And he shall come again with glory to judge both the quick and the dead: Whose kingdom shall have no end.

And I believe in the Holy Ghost, the Lord and giver of life, Who proceedeth from the Father and the Son, Who with the Father and the Son together is worshipped and glorified, Who spake by the Prophets. And I believe one Catholick and Apostolick Church. I acknowledge one Baptism for the remission of sins. And I look for the Resurrection of the dead, And the life of the world to come.

A creed was first drawn up at a council of fourth-century Christian leaders which had been convened by the Roman Emperor Constantine to settle a bitter theological feud. It can be argued that Constantine's interest in the matter was not so much theological as political. He wanted a unified religion for the Empire, preferably under centralized, Roman control. He had become Christian, so the legend recounts, as a result of a vision. On the eve of the battle at which he captured Rome and took power, Constantine saw the Christian symbol and the words, 'By this sign, you shall be the victor'.

On achieving power, the new emperor proceeded to reverse the policy of persecution towards the Christians. Not that he became a pious and humble follower of the Carpenter of Nazareth in his personal life, and he continued long after conversion to murder political opponents and members of his family. He also mixed Christianity with the pagan Sol Invictus cult. He did however seek baptism and renounced the Imperial purple at the end of his life.

The theological feud which Constantine found himself obliged to referee concerned the exact understanding Christians should have of Jesus as God. To put the argument in its crudest form, Was the Jesus who became man also one and the same person with God the creator who had always been? To Arius, the Son had been created by God at the time of his mission on earth. To Athanasius and Bishop Alexander of Alexandria this view was to make Jesus appear less than God, and this could not be so.

So deep was the rift caused by the argument that Constantine summoned a Council of Christians to resolve it once and for all. It was a gathering of holy men from all corners of Asia and Europe reached by the new faith. Many of those attending, like Bishop Pamphnutius, had been victims of the earlier persecution. Jacob, the hermit of Nisibis, came clad in a filthy goatskin. There was Nicholas of Myra, representatives of the Bishop of Rome and of course Arius.

Constantine himself was no theologian but possessed good political instincts. He cajoled and persuaded and in some instances leant on the delegates to all sign a unified declaration of faith.

In his book accompanying the controversial 'Jesus: the Evidence' television programme broadcast shortly before David Jenkins' 'Credo' appearance, the historian Ian Wilson describes the conclusion to the Council like this:

Constantine urged all Council delegates to sign the revised formula as a statement of faith on which all Christians should in future agree. For all those who signed, there was the inducement of an invitation to stay on at Nicaea as Constantine's guests for his twentieth anniversary celebrations. For those who refused there was immediate banishment. Among all concerned, it appears to have gone entirely unnoticed that the formula they were about to impose on all Christians contained not one jot of the ethical teachings that the human Jesus had once preached. Perhaps not unexpectedly, all but two of the most die-hard Arian loyalists signed. But, from the none too truthful face-saving letter Eusebius of Caesarea sent back to his home diocese, it is clear how uneasy he felt about the extent to which he had compromised the fundamental principles of what he had been taught about Jesus. Other signatories, who were equally swayed into acquiescence by their awe of the forceful Constantine, felt exactly the same. Only on returning home did Eusebius of Nicomedia, Maris of Chalcedon and Theognis of Nicaea summon the courage to express to Constantine in writing how much they regretted having put their signature on the Nicene formula: 'We committed an impious act, O Prince,' wrote Eusebius of Nicomedia, 'by subscribing to a blasphemy from fear of you.'

But it was too late. An overwhelming majority of Christianity's highest dignitaries had put pen to parchment, and even though the Arian controversy would rumble on for another two or three centuries, effectively there was no turning back. Although no Gospel regarded Jesus as God and not even Paul had done so, the Jewish teacher had been declared Very God through all eternity, and a whole theology would flow from this.

The creed backed by Constantine was the subject of fierce controversy for more than fifty years. In the end, under the watchful eye of Emperor Theodosius, a creed was drawn up in Constantinople in 381 to settle the matter. This is the creed we call the Nicene Creed (which should really be called the Nicaeno-Constantinopolitan Creed, but this is rather a mouthful). It has held the field for more than a thousand years. With the reformation came a challenge to the centralized Roman control of much of Christendom which had survived since the days of the Roman Empire; and with the 'modern' theologians, three hundred years later, came the challenge to the doctrinal formula.

While Constantine's political manoeuvring had produced much of what we recognize as familiar in Christianity today and while the Council of Nicaea was crucial in crystallizing the dogmas concerning the virgin birth and the resurrection, it must be pointed out that the belief in the miraculous events surrounding Christ's birth and raising from the dead was established well before the fourth century A.D.

This point was made by three academics, Anglican teachers of theology at Durham University, who wrote to the Archbishop of York following the Archbishop's letter to Mr Ledwich replying to the petition.

The content of both Scripture and the Creeds unambiguously affirms both a miraculous conception and a bodily resurrection of Our Lord. The Fathers of the Church before the division of East and West kept the Creeds relatively short, including only those beliefs that they held to be essential to a true faith. These beliefs included the miracles of the Virgin Birth and Empty Tomb – for all the speculation in which theologians of the period indulged, there was no questioning of either doctrine in the early Church which was not immediately declared heretical.

Thus in the second century, Gnosticism proclaimed an experience of resurrection divorced from a bodily resurrection, and the Catholic Church condemned this idea as strongly as any other heresy was condemned. The gnostic contempt for bodily existence involved denial of the redemption of the whole of Christ's humanity and our own. In the second century, that great Bishop and Theologian, St Irenaeus, spent nearly the whole of Book Five of his major work, *Adversus Haereses*, refuting views analogous to those recently put forward by Bishop Jenkins.

St Irenaeus has been held in the highest regard throughout Christian tradition, Orthodox, Roman Catholic, Protestant and Anglican. By contrast the 1938 Report on Doctrine, a belated product of the erosion of Christian belief under the onslaught of Enlightenment, tried to paper over the cracks caused by the reassertion in the Church of heterodox doctrine by cautiously affirming a liberty of interpretation.

In effect the Church of England in 1938 seemed prepared to declare null and void the outcome of the debates of the early Church which led to the formulation of the historic creeds. However, although the 1938 Report on Doctrine was 'received' by the Church, moves to use it as the basis for a modern restatement of doctrine were wisely rejected and it remains entirely unofficial.

While doctrinal matters which have lain dormant for centuries can come to life again, often new generations find they have new stumbling blocks to a full acceptance of the Christian faith and tradition; ones which would not have occurred to the faithful in a former age perhaps. For what appears an insurmountable problem to one generation or community will appear to another to be quite a peripheral matter. Who in twentieth-century European society today, for instance, is much bothered by the medieval debate as to how many angels could dance on the end of a pin?

In the 1960s David Jenkins was much involved in questioning the old and seeking for new images for God, as part of the 'Honest to God' debate. *Honest to God* was the work of John Robinson, then Bishop of Woolwich, who did much to set his generation thinking about how to visualize the Almighty.

If the simplistic picture of God, an old benevolent gentleman with long white beard sitting on a throne, is abandoned, an alternative set of images has to be found. Finding these new images is something David Jenkins has not found easy. Most human beings need some form of rudimentary image which they can use to form some understanding of that which is beyond human understanding; finding images adequate to the task is very difficult.

Writer and lawyer, John Mortimer, received a very unsatisfactory answer when he threw David Jenkins the question, 'What is God?'

There was a silence,' John Mortimer wrote, recalling the occasion:

The Bishop's legs shot out, his fingertips met, he searched for elusive words. Could it be that the question was as troubling to him as it was to me?

'I think . . . Yes!' The words seemed to hover in the air and he swooped on them. 'He is the power behind all things. He is present in all things. He is the promise of all things.'

'Is He a personal God?'

'Not ultra-personalised.' The bishop looked anxiously at his highly polished shoes and suddenly became more cheerful. 'I got into trouble recently for calling God "He, She or It".'

'Is He, She or It omnipotent?'

The Bishop blinked unhappily at the word. 'Let's say, there are no limits to His power.' From then on the 'She' and 'It' dropped quietly from the conversation.

In explaining his understanding of God, David Jenkins admits he is no poet. As a result, his self-confessed inadequate expression of what he feels, knows and understands of God, lays him open to many criticisms. He can easily be attacked by those who do not share or comprehend his fumbling imagery.

Perhaps it has been the problem throughout the ages that people have argued over the imagery, which can at best be but a poor substitute for the reality, without stopping to realize that they, in fact, share the same knowledge of God, and that problems arise because they express that same knowledge in different ways. It is like two people, speaking different languages, trying to have a conversation. They get angry and frustrated with each other, not because they hold diametrically opposed views but because they cannot share with each other the views they hold in common.

8

'Is it your will that he should be ordained?'

When the day came for the consecration, there was a tension in the air at the Minster. Legal threats to cancel the service had been withdrawn but there still remained the fear that protesters could infiltrate the congregation and cause considerable disruption, destroying both the joy and solemnity of the occasion.

The legal threat had centred around the taking, by David Jenkins, of the solemn oath of canonical obedience. The Reverand David Holloway had sought the advice of a church laywer who said that if David Jenkins continued to hold his present views after being made a bishop he would be breaking that oath as he would be contravening one of the canons, the laws, of the Church. Canon 18 reads, 'every bishop is . . . to uphold sound and wholesome doctrine, and to banish and drive away all erroneous and strange opinions; and to set forward and maintain quietness, love and peace among all men.' And what is sound and wholesome doctrine? The answer is to be found in Canon A5.

The doctrine of the Church of England is grounded in the Holy Scriptures and in such teachings of the ancient Fathers and Councils of the Church as are agreeable to the said Scripture. In particular such doctrine is to be found in the thirty-nine Articles of Religion, the Book of Common Prayer and the Ordinal.

And the thirty-nine Articles found in the old 1662 Prayer

Book, David Holloway argued, are quite clear in their belief in the fact of the virgin birth and the resurrection.

The Archbishop of York chose to overlook David Holloway's reasoning and continued with the consecration as planned, even though it was pointed out to him that there was nothing in statute or common law to prevent him from refusing the Crown's appointee.

Legal appeals having failed, the opponents were left only with unofficial avenues of protest.

As the 2,000-strong invited congregation arrived at the Minster for the consecration they found a handful of protesters outside with placards. One quoted Isaiah, 'A virgin shall conceive'. In the event the consecration was interrupted twice in two hours. Just before the sermon, which was preached by Professor Dennis Nineham, a man who said that his name was Barry, shouted, 'This is invalid,' and 'Let no more denigration be brought on Jesus Christ.' He was almost immediately escorted out of the Minster by two vergers.

The second interruption was a far more substantial affair. The Vicar of Buglawton, near Congleton in Cheshire, the Reverend John Mowll, presented himself at the lectern as the Royal Mandate was being read. It was a premeditated interruption of the service and he began to read a prepared statement. He had only read the first few sentences before stewards and a plain-clothes police officer tugged him by the jacket and hustled him from the rostrum and out of the Cathedral. There were a few shouts of 'shame' from the congregation. He was frog-marched, protesting, out of the Minster. Because the public-address system was not working, few heard Mr Mowll's protest in the Minster, but he distributed a leaflet containing his statement to make sure the message was not entirely lost. It read:

The Christian faith is about what we as Christians believe. Not to believe in the Virgin Birth and in the Resurrection of our Lord as facts of history is a very grave matter for anyone. How much more so for a man who is about to make solemn vows before God and to be consecrated as a bishop in the Church of England which has its standards of faith in the thirty-nine Articles of Religion and the Book of Common Prayer, in the historic Creeds of the Church, and above all, in the Bible, where the apostles gave clear and unequivocal witness to these historic facts, just as the Church has always received them.

That a would-be bishop who should be a guardian and teacher of the Christian faith is one known to deny these to have in fact happened – thus removing the basis for the two most important doctrines about our Lord which make him unique – is perhaps, in the realm of faith, the greatest blasphemy possible.

That the Church can be party to such a thing will, in the eyes of all honest people, deny it the right to speak out on any moral or ethical issue.

I beg you to play with words no longer, because this will bring great shame to the Church throughout the world, and to take no further part in this service. I invite you to follow me out of this Church as a timely protest against what is happening, or about to happen, and as a protest in favour of the truth.

Mr Mowll's protest ensured him notoriety but he found little support in the Cathedral. The only people to follow him out were the stewards to make sure he stayed out.

The service of consecration continued as planned, with the Archbishop of York saying to the people, 'Those who have authority to do so have chosen David Edward Jenkins as a man of godly life and sound learning, to be a bishop in the Church of God. Is it therefore your will that he should be ordained?'

There was a resounding reply of 'It is'. And the Archbishop continued, 'Will you uphold him in his ministry?' Back came the reply, 'We will'. There were no dissenters audible. The consecration proceeded in the grey-speak of the Alternative Service Book which has now, by and large, in the upper echelons of Anglicanism, replaced the beautiful sixteenth-century prose of the Book of Common Prayer.

The Archbishop read the preface to the declaration of assent:

'The Church of England is part of the one, holy, catholic, and apostolic Church, worshipping the one true God, Father, Son, and Holy Spirit. It professes the faith uniquely revealed in the holy Scriptures and set forth in the catholic creeds, which faith the Church is called upon to proclaim afresh in each generation. Led by the Holy Spirit, it has borne witness to Christian truth in its historic formularies, the Thirty-nine Articles of Religion, the Book of Common Prayer, and the Ordering of Bishops, Priests, and Deacons. In the declaration you are about to make, will you affirm your loyalty to this inheritance of faith as your inspiration and guidance under God in bringing the grace and truth of Christ to this generation and making him known to those in your care?'

At which question the point in the service had arrived which required David Jenkins to make a personal affirmation. It was an affirmation which he could make in all conscience, according to his own interpretations and understandings, but one which his opponents believed he could only make in hypocrisy and dishonesty.

'I, David Edward Jenkins, do so affirm, and accordingly declare my belief in the faith which is revealed in the holy Scriptures and set forth in the catholic creeds and to which the historic formularies of the Church of England bear witness, and in public prayer and administration of the sacraments, I will use only the forms of service which are authorized or allowed by Canon.'

With the bishop-elect standing before the Archbishop and with the people sitting, the Archbishop then outlined the duties of a bishop and questioned him on his suitability. In his reply to the petitioners, the Archbishop of York had drawn attention to the public declarations expected from David Jenkins. In the Minster the bishop-elect made them in a clear unequivocal voice. The Archbishop asked him:

'Do you accept the holy Scriptures as revealing all things necessary for eternal salvation through faith in Jesus Christ?'

DAVID JENKINS: I do so accept them.

ARCHBISHOP: Do you believe the doctrine of the Christian faith as the Church of England has received it, and in your ministry will you expound and teach it?

DAVID JENKINS: I believe it and will do so.

ARCHBISHOP: Will you accept the discipline of this Church, and faithfully exercise authority within it?

DAVID JENKINS: By the help of God, I will.

ARCHBSISHOP: Will you be diligent in prayer, in reading holy Scripture, and in all studies that will deepen your faith and fit you to uphold the truth of the Gospel against error?

DAVID JENKINS: By the help of God, I will.

ARCHBISHOP: Will you strive to fashion your own life and that of your household according to the way of Christ?

DAVID JENKINS: By the help of God, I will.

ARCHBISHOP: Will you promote unity, peace, and love

71

among all Christian people, and especially among those whom you serve?

DAVID JENKINS: By the help of God, I will.

ARCHBISHOP: Will you then be a faithful witness to Christ to those among whom you live, and lead your people to obey our Saviour's commands to make disciples of all nations?

DAVID JENKINS: By the help of God I will.

The ordination itself took place when, after praying, amongst other things, to be delivered from error and false doctrine, and that God's ministers be enlightened with knowledge and understanding to proclaim the word by their teaching, all the bishops present joined the Archbishop, and the bishop-elect knelt in front of them. They laid their hands on David Jenkins' head and ordained him by name. Then the Archbishop continued:

'Through him increase your Church, renew its ministry, and unite its members in a holy fellowship of truth and love. Enable him as a true shepherd to feed and govern your flock; make him wise as a teacher, and steadfast as a guardian of its faith and sacraments. Guide and direct him in presiding at the worship of your people. Give him humility, that he may use his authority to heal, not to hurt; to build up, not to destroy.'

And then, in what must have been seen by the opponents to be the final irony of hypocrisy, the new Bishop David Jenkins was presented with a Bible, the book whose authority and absolute reliability, he appeared to challenge.

'Receive this Book; here are words of eternal life. Take them for your guide, and declare them to the world. Keep

72

watch over the whole flock in which the Holy Spirit has appointed you shepherd. Encourage the faithful, restore the lost, build up the body of Christ; that when the Chief Shepherd shall appear, you may receive the unfading crown of glory.'

At the end of the Eucharist which concluded the service of consecration there was one final unscheduled disruption, but one which neither the new bishop nor Archbishop minded. Applause rang through the Minster for nearly two minutes as they left the nave, an almost unprecedented gesture of support and goodwill from the people.

It was early the next Monday morning, with the Minster silent and empty, that lightning struck the building. William Ledwich, whose petition the Archbishop had rejected and who had decided with much sorrow to leave the Church of England for the Orthodox Church, was to write later of the fire:

It would obviously be impossible to say that it was God's direct intervention; it would be equally wrong to assert that it was not. We shall never know . . . We know nothing. What is remarkable, however, is that on David Jenkins' definition of a miracle, it was a miracle. For he sees a miracle as an ordinary natural event which people use to illustrate a theological point. Many, many people saw it in some way connected with the events of the previous weekend. We cannot say that God did not strike the Minster, for who are we to limit the way in which God speaks to us? At any rate it became a real and deeply felt symbol for the multitudes of faithful Christians who wanted to say very clearly that the Consecration of David Jenkins in the light of his express heresy, and such clear warning, was a wicked and profane act, which God would not condone.'

9

The Synod debate

It so happened that the Synod, the Church of England parliament, was due to meet in York in the week of the fire.

Exactly twenty-four hours after the Minster had been packed with Synod members for the Sunday Eucharist, the Archbishop of Canterbury found himself back in the building under very different circumstances. A hard-hat had replaced his mitre as he stood against the charred timbers beneath the blackened rose window. He quickly disposed of any notion that the lightning bolt which had fired the Minster had been the work of a revengeful God, angered over the elevation of David Jenkins to the Bishopric of Durham. Dr Runcie said he was at the Minster to convey the sympathy of the whole Synod to the Dean and Chapter. He had never seen such destruction he said since seeing the ruined cathedrals of Cologne and Rouen during the war. From Monday onwards talk of the fire dominated the Synod. On the previous Saturday however, the opening day, the consecration itself had been the main talking point.

The Reverend David Holloway, who had previously gone to considerable lengths to explore legal grounds for deferring the consecration, led the case for the opponents in the debate. He suggested to the Synod that they should begin their deliberation with a two-minute period of silent prayer.

He said that the debate should not be centred on the new bishop but was about the fundamental doctrines of the Church of England. David Jenkins, he said, had simply been the 'catalyst for issues that had lain under the surface for a long time'.

The *Church Times* reported Mr Holloway's case extensively. The whole issue hinged on two questions:

First, was the Church of England going to remain firmly part of the one, holy, Catholic and apostolic Church? And secondly, who was going to decide?

Something had to be done; and, 'if the initiative does not come from the top, it is bound to come from the bottom. There's a limit to "comprehensiveness" and "inclusiveness". And the church on the ground is saying, "We have reached that limit".'

The gospel, Mr Holloway stressed, not only witnessed to different insights to the mystery – it also distinguished truth from error; many people were convinced intellectually that historic Christianity was true and that the views of Bishop Jenkins were false. But who was to decide?

The Church he was in, whose bishops they looked to for doctrinal leadership, was the Church disciplined and determined by measures, canons and other instruments. 'None of us wish to be legalists. But, in matters of dispute, the canons of the Church of England must be our arbiter. And, in matters of doctrinal dispute, the canons are binding . . . And they are binding on archbishops and bishops as well as on the inferior clergy.'

Mr Holloway went on: 'The question before us now is this: can the episcopate, or individual members of it, be over, or must they all be under, the canons? The answer is, surely, this. The episcopate, to which we can in conscience give allegiance, is only the episcopate as it acts within the Church of England as by law established and therefore under canon.

'I submit that two minutes' adjournment for prayer and recollection, whatever view we may take of this matter, whatever side we may take, would be an appropriate Christian response to the seriousness of this situation the Church is in. If the General Synod doesn't recognize it, the country certainly does. This is a very, very, crucial matter.'

Some members clapped vigorously as Mr Holloway sat down; but it was noticeable that more members pointedly refrained from applauding.

The Archbishop of York replied that while he would welcome a full debate on the issues at some time, he did not think that that was the most appropriate time. He also asked Synod to reject the idea of a two-minute silence as a 'totally wrong use of prayer within the synodical business'. By a show of hands Mr Holloway's proposal was lost.

Despite his frustration with the hierarchy of the Church of England, David Holloway decided to remain an Anglican and fight from within. He and Tony Higton have used a variety of official and unofficial devices to keep the debate alive. In their view the claim that the Jenkins' heresy is the ascendant view amongst the powers that be in the Church has been given additional credence with every uttering from Bishopthorpe.

It was there, amidst the palatial splendours of his residence, that the Archbishop of York, under questioning on BBC Radio 4, was pushed into admitting his views on the resurrection. 'Speaking purely historically, I don't believe that one can dig down and find a definitive answer.' The facts 'were totally inaccessible to historical investigation'.

He took the opportunity in his July 1984 diocesan leaflet to give his views more substance. Theology, he said was in the news again. The public discussion being maintained on television and in the press had revealed how difficult it was for the general Christian public to appreciate what theologians were doing. He therefore would look at the question of the virgin birth as an example of the subtle interplay between various levels of belief:

The starting point for understanding any theology is the frank recognition that theologians are trying to do the impossible. Human language, however sophisticated or exalted, is inadequate to describe the mystery and splendour of God. This is why various types of language have to be used – straight historical narrative, poetry, parable, exhortation, complex symbolism, in fact every available device for stretching words and images far beyond their normal meaning. To confuse these different types of language, to treat poetry as history, say, or vice versa, is to create unnecessary difficulties. But even if that pitfall is avoided, words in the end must fail. All true theology culminates in the prayer of silent adoration. And it is in such prayer that different expressions of theological truth may come to be seen as not necessarily in conflict, but complementing and correcting one another.

The Creeds, which try to catch in words the essence of the Christian faith as it was defined in relation to particular historical conflict, stand as permanent signposts of Christian orthodoxy. But in interpreting them the same principle applies as in interpreting the Scriptures on which they are based. Each generation of Christians has to use the best scholarship available to get back into the minds of those who first experienced the impact of Christ's coming, and endeavoured to put it into words, and then ask the question, 'What must the truth have been if it appeared like this to men who thought and spoke like that?' The terms in which the truth is expressed may differ in different generations. The essential thing, and the true test of orthodoxy, is not whether we would use this or that precise form of words if we were writing the creeds today, but whether through them we can discern the authentic vision and experience to which they bear witness.

So with that as a preliminary, and very compressed, warning about what to expect of theology, let me turn to the doctrines of the virgin birth. Why is it in the creed, and what is its importance?

The first essential is to be clear about the logical relation between this doctrine and the doctrine of the incarnation. Many people mistakenly suppose that belief in the incarnation somehow depends on belief in the virgin birth. In the New Testament, however, the overwhelming emphasis is on the resurrection of Jesus, and the continuing evidence of his presence, and his fulfilment of the purposes of God as Christians came to understand these from the Old Testament. It is the whole impact of his life, death and victory over death, which drives forward the belief that here indeed is the ultimate revelation of God's presence. The virgin birth came to be seen as a fitting expression of this truth, but it can hardly have been central to New Testament thought, since the majority of New Testament writers make no mention of it. It follows that doubts about the virgin birth do not necessarily imply doubts about the incarnation, though obviously the fact that it occurs in the creed means that it came to be regarded as having a special importance. What was this?

There are many possible explanations. The emphasis on the birth of Jesus from a human mother was a safeguard against a heresy known as 'docetism', the belief that Jesus was not really a man at all, but merely God 'appearing' as man. The emphasis on the work of the Holy Spirit in the conception of Jesus highlights the new beginning for humanity, the new work of God promised in the Old Testament, now inaugurated in the coming of Christ. There is a more subtle theological point being made also in terms of the transition from Judaism to Christianity. Judaism, though potentially a universal religion in its scope, was and is heavily dependent on actual physical heredity. Most Jews are born Jews. Christianity broke out of this mould to become truly universal, and the breaking of the physical heredity in its origins is a powerful symbol of this universality.

These are some of the theological reasons why those who first experienced the newness of life in Christ felt it appropriate to express it through this article in the creed. There may also have been less desirable theological motives, among them the revulsion from current attitudes towards sex, and the consequent exaltation of virginity. Some would question the doctrine as threatening belief in the true manhood of Christ. There is also a dangerous streak in all new and exciting religious experience which accentuates marvels and tries to use these, often unwisely, as if they were the main evidence for the experience itself.

Some contemporary theologians are more concerned about these negative aspects of the doctrine than its positive value in symbolizing God's new initiative. Inevitably this affects their interpretation of the historical evidence.

I come to the question of history last because, in the nature of the case, the historical evidence is bound to be very slender. Apart from a few possible, and disputed, hints in St John's Gospel and two Pauline epistles, the sole evidence is in the nativity stories in Matthew and Luke. The fact that these differ from one another, while agreeing on the fundamental point, is an indication that the tradition on which they are based is older than both of them; this is a fairly strong reason for believing that they are witnessing to a real historical event. But the most important point is that, for the purpose of Christian faith, it is what a doctrine tells us about God that matters, rather than whether it is possible to make firm historical judgements about an event which is by its nature inaccessible to ordinary investigation.

In summary, therefore, the structure of theological thinking on the subject is something like this:

As Christians we believe that God has done a new thing in Jesus Christ, revealing himself in a human life, subject to the ordinary conditions of humanity. The historical reality of this new thing is attested by the New Testament and by two thousand years of Christian experience.

The doctrine of the virgin birth is a powerful symbol of this truth, but is not the only means by which the truth can be expressed or safeguarded.

Evaluation of the doctrine has to rely more on judgements about its theological appropriateness than on historical study.

This is only a very small sketch map of a large territory, but I hope it may help some of those who are puzzled by recent public discussion of these matters.

It was a statement far short of an unequivocal belief in the virgin birth as a fact which many traditionalists would have hoped for but a comprehensive statement of the new orthodoxy in the Church.

10

The media and the message

'I'm going to do a Brer Rabbit now and lie low.' If, by uttering those words shortly after his consecration, David Jenkins thought that he would be able to fade into episcopal obscurity, he was very wrong. He was in a position where almost anything he said was widely reported, and as he was tackling his notoriety with some relish it was very unlikely that the new Bishop Jenkins would be out of the headlines for long.

Fleet Street has a habit of making the most of those they view as maverick prelates. At the time of David Jenkins' appointment there was somewhat of a dearth of colourful bishops and deans. No longer was Bishop Robinson at Woolwich or the Red Dean at Canterbury: even Mervyn Stockwood had left Southwark for retirement in Bath. There were a few bishops like Birmingham and Edmonton, later Petersborough, who were media-conscious. The Bishop of London was deemed quotable by Fleet Street but generally only as a type-cast conservative. As to the Archbishops, neither had captured the imagination of the press. The Archbishop of Canterbury had made a stir by not rejoicing to order at the Falklands service, but had been criticized by many for not sticking his head above the parapet until the war was over.

Certain bishops were held in high respect by the opinion-setters of the media – David Sheppard at Liverpool and John Taylor at Winchester in particular. They handled the press with a careful courtesy, being prepared to commit themselves to print or tape only when they had something positive, original and constructive to say. They were therefore not Fleet Street favourites, especially as Liverpool had successfully distanced himself from his cricketing past. Who under the age of thirty now knows he used to be England's captain?

The field was therefore open for a new lively, high-ranking cleric to make a name for himself. David Jenkins was seized upon as a God-given gift to the business of ephemeral writing.

For all the confusion which can exist in his prose, David Jenkins does have a knack of turning the memorable phrase. Whether he knows in advance which phrases will be quotable and which not is unlikely, but he talks at such speed that by the law of chance a well coined and pithy remark is bound to appear in the course of his speaking.

He has still much to learn about how best to present himself on the air, but in newsprint his style of communicating ideas works well. It was one single sentence which, in the eyes of the media, made his enthronement sermon memorable. That however was not scheduled to take place until September. In the meantime David Jenkins had to familiarize himself with diocesan matters, deal with the voluminous correspondence his remarks had attracted and fit in a growing number of public engagements. It soon became apparent too that he had uncovered deep-seated insecurities of faith in a number of people who reacted with a personally directed loathing. Hate mail arrived at the bishop's new home, the majestic castle at Bishop Auckland. There was even a death threat made and the fact that it came to nothing did little to diminish the shock of being on the receiving end of such venom. David Jenkins was later to reflect on the probable sociological and psychological significance of the reaction he received, especially in connection with the York Minster fire.

'It brought out how strongly a "primitive" belief in an

arbitrary and vengeful God who exercises supernatural (magical?) powers is alive (if not well!).

'As one who has long been clear, both as a matter of simple observation and as part of a Christian understanding of God, men and women and the world, that everybody sins and religious people sin religiously, I have not found the controversy to have totally unexpected aspects nor have I found it too upsetting, but there are one or two features which are certainly disturbing. The first and most obvious is the extraordinary way in which people seem to believe newspaper headlines or short newspaper reports. Of course, one has long known this in theory, but to have personal knowledge of how reports start by being misleading and end up by being quite untrue, combined with personal knowledge of indignant or distressed accusations starting from such untrue or grossly simplified reports, is to be reminded very sharply of how credulous and uncritical people are. How quickly, therefore, could highly organized propaganda manipulate, and what a distorted and limited view of the world must be the basis of action and reaction by so many voters! The price of any sort of liberty would seem to be eternal suspicion. But will enough people be prepared to pay the price and will they have enough effect?

'This disturbing personal experience of the trivializing of truth by the media is matched by equally disturbing evidence of an absence of a concern for truth among the self-styled defenders of Christian faith and orthodoxy. Among the articles known to me and in the letters received by me there was hardly any discussion of the case for holding that what I said was true. The discussion almost wholly centred round whether I, as a bishop-designate, should say such things, I even received letters from quite respectable and senior clergymen, which suggested that a professor of theology (who was a believing Christian) was quite entitled to pursue such questions in such a way, but a bishop was not. I felt obliged to reply to at least two such

84

writers that their suggestion seemed to me to be, from the point of view of Christian faith in God, precious close to blasphemy and, from the point of view of simple human logic, identical with nonsense. On the one hand the pursuit of truth was to be suppressed or ignored in the interests of a responsibility to God and his Church, on the other a mere shift of institutional responsibility apparently justified two different and incompatible sets of truth values and criteria for truth.'

On the occasions David Jenkins was confronted by opponents in person his style was equally robust. On a 'phone-in' on the London commercial radio station L.B.C, the Bishop was involved in an angry exchange with a caller from New Malden in Surrey. The caller, identified as is normal on an L.B.C. phone-in by his Christian name only, said that he was an Anglican religious-education and Sunday-school teacher.

David, the caller, had hardly started to put his question when David, the bishop, started a series of interruptions.

'I don't think it's fair to keep chipping in like that,' David, the caller, protested. He was trying to make the point that many young people were disgusted with the Bishop's denial of what he saw as key teachings.

'I do believe in the resurrection. I've said it again and again. You have misunderstood what I said,' the Bishop snapped. He said that Christ's resurrection body was 'spiritual', it could after all go through doors. Of the reported empty tomb Bishop Jenkins said, 'There's one explanation in Matthew, that the disciples came and pinched the body. We can't be sure about it, can we?

'The only thing we can be sure about is that the personality and presence and power in the spiritual body of Jesus so impressed people that they have been convinced ever since he was alive.'

Bishop Jenkins gave short shrift to another caller,

Marjorie, who tried to make the point that both Matthew and Luke were quite clear that Mary, the mother of Jesus, was a virgin.

'It's not a newspaper report, is it? It is a story which is being told about a generation or two generations after the event.' And after a further prickly exchange he said, 'I'm not taking the Bible literally because it cannot be taken literally. You're being medieval about it, I'm afraid, Madam!'

'You're the Anti-Christ,' Marjorie replied!

Of course not all reaction was hostile and at one stage a count revealed that of the 1,500 letters sent to David Jenkins, supporters outweighed opponents by a ratio of nearly three-to-one.

Of the published letters of support a number were written by people who had known David Jenkins personally and who did not recognize in David Jenkins, the media image, the same man they knew. The Vicar of St Chad's at Headingley in Leeds, the Reverend Brian Abell, wrote to the *Yorkshire Post* at the end of May to say how many members of his church had been upset by what they read of David Jenkins in the press. Professor Jenkins had worked in the parish as priest combining parochial duties with his academic commitments. Brian Abell wrote:

David Jenkins is known to us above all as a man of great faith and devotion. Criticisms of his remarks on a TV programme show, first, a lack of understanding of the difficulty of communicating in a balanced way in the media and, second, a neurotic desire for 'certainty'.

The kind of certainty such people seek is fraudulent, must be resisted and is due to a lack of security – not trust in God. We have seen in David the great gift of encouraging others in the open and continuing search for belief.

Accusations of 'heresy' by those who should know better have been clearly answered by David's recent statement and should not have been necessary for a man who has contributed so much to theological understanding and dialogue.

We thank God for him, think Durham is very fortunate and know that the vast majority of people there will welcome and come to love and respect him as we do as a real Christian man of integrity and faith.

And one of his parishioners, Gill Pitchford of Headingley, came to David Jenkins' defence on the *Church Times* letters page on 1 June. She said of his preaching:

Listening to him, I, a decidedly 'run-of-the-mill', non-intellectual and often hesitant Christian, have been informed, amused and surely most important of all, inspired to carry on exploring Christianity as a dynamic, joyful and relevant way of living life in this latter half of the twentieth century. No doubt he will do the same, and much more, for the people of Durham.

I'm not aware that Christ enjoined us to agree with one another all of the time; but he did suggest we might love one another. I trust that Durham will love and enjoy their new Bishop.

A week later a letter from Mrs Winifred Crook of Southampton appeared in the same paper.

Can it not be believed that the choice of a new Bishop for Durham is an answer to prayer that a right choice should be made? That the one chosen, a firm believer in the Holy Trinity, will guide us toward a deeper knowledge of the God we profess to worship?

As the summer progressed there were still those who could not let the question of a 'heretical' bishop rest. Tony

Higton's newly formed Action for Biblical Witness to our Nation and David Holloway and others now set their sights on ensuring that no similar appointment would be made again. David Holloway was much involved at the September meeting of the North East Diocesan Evangelical Fellowship.

It was there an idea gained support to test bishops at a parish level. The Fellowship decided to encourage parishes throughout Britain to think about asking bishops, before they proceed to conduct confirmation, or exercise any other ministry in a local church, to subscribe to the declaration of belief: 'I believe in the fact of the Virgin Birth of Jesus Christ and his Resurrection on the third day from the tomb as is clearly taught in the Holy Scriptures.' There were forty-five clergy present plus senior laymen and the meeting voted

> its deep concern that the Archbishop of York, and a significant number of Bishops, in relation to the consecration of the new bishop, had by word and action declared as optional belief in the Virgin Birth of Jesus Christ and his Resurrection on the third day from the tomb; such teaching is not compatible with the faith of the one, holy, catholic and apostolic Church nor the teaching of the Church of England as by law established.
>
> There is no way that churches will grow when there is doctrinal confusion . . . We are strongly convinced [the meeting voted] that the urgent need in the North East is for local churches to be strengthened and to grow. The North East has witnessed a decline in Church attendance over the 100 years. The clergy need renewed vision, confidence and hope in God and the Gospel of Jesus Christ. Denials of, or doubts over, fundamental doctrines by Bishops are demotivating. The current situation in society at large, evidenced by the present violence and disagreement in our industrial sectors in the North East demonstrate a vacuum of spiritual values and spiritual

direction in the Nation. Doubts, uncertainties and errors expressed by Bishops add to that vacuum.

The reference to the violence and disagreement in the industrial sector was a reference to the secular topic which dominated the British news in 1984 – the miners' strike. Two-thirds of the National Union of Mineworkers had answered the call of the President, Arthur Scargill, and staged a strike to save what was described as a hit list of pits being closed and many thousands of miners being made redundant. It was the policy of the National Coal Board, under its new Scottish-born American Chairman, Ian MacGregor, to prune the industry cutting out all uneconomic pits. What constituted an uneconomic pit was however hotly disputed. The strike took many bitter turns and when miners tried to picket mines in strength to prevent dissident members from working, the police were used in such a way that relations between the force and the mining community became tense and violent. In some pit villages police stations were attacked, and on the picket lines many officers armed in riot gear meted out brutal treatment.

David Jenkins, through his work with the William Temple Foundation and his study of Marxism, was no stranger to grappling with political matters as they related to belief. He had also decided to become involved in and identify himself with the community of his diocese, and his diocese contained an active, but threatened, coal-mining industry.

He therefore took up the challenge of the North East Diocesan Evangelical Fellowship in his enthronement sermon, but not in quite the way they would have wished.

11

'Imported, elderly American'

One three-word phrase ensured that Bishop Jenkins'
enthronement sermon would not go unnoticed. He
described the Chairman of the National Coal Board as an
'imported, elderly American'.

Apart from the factual inaccuracy of the description, for
such an overtly political thought to be aired in a new
bishop's introductory address to his diocese was unusual.
It was not unprecedented; bishops have engaged in political
debate on many occasions but not often so early in their
episcopates. Thanks, too, to David Jenkins' newly acquired
status with the media he could be assured of a wide public.

The sermon in its entirety is a *tour de force* full of typical
Jenkins' vigour and provocation. It was designed to make
the congregation sit up and listen. It is full of quotable
passages, any one of which could have made the headlines.
The media however prefers issues to be personalized. One
of the reasons the subtleties of theology are hard to convey
in newsprint is that abstract ideas are not so easily reported
in journalese as are clashes of personality. So it was that
David Jenkins' carefully crafted sentences on 'the glimpse
of glory in the Transfiguration' and the 'fulfilling of the
transfiguring glory' in 'the disfiguring of the cross' were
largely overlooked by the reporters present in the great
Norman cathedral. They were interested in what they saw
as the broadside fired at Mr Ian MacGregor.

It is also fair to say that the press was hoping for a new
'angle' from the bishop. The theological row had, in media

terms, almost run out of steam. It was hoped the bishop might breathe new life into the controversy in his sermon by introducing a new twist. For him to choose to weigh in to the current main political issue was both unexpected and welcomed.

David Jenkins took as his text Romans, chapter 15, verse 13: 'May the God of hope fill you with all joy and peace by your faith in him, until by the power of the Holy Spirit, you overflow with hope.'

'We could do with some help from this "God of Hope" here in the north-east. Unemployment is at 35 to 50 per cent. They propose to dump radioactive waste on us as if we were the scrap-yard of Britain. The miners' strike highlights how divided and distressed society is, to the point of violence. Christians seem absorbed in bad-tempered arguments about belief, or marriage or politics. The organized Churches find financial problems looming larger and larger. We all wonder if the old men in the Kremlin or in the White House will overreach themselves and actually use the nuclear weapons which are unthinkable but real. If you stop and think, hope does not come easily.'

Having reflected on the fact that he was not everyone's 'cup of tea' and had even been accused of being some people's cup of poison, David Jenkins then mused over his title and territorial responsibilities:

'The Bishop will stand for and serve the whole of the County of Durham, indeed, the whole of the north-east . . . If such opportunities for service and representation are open to me, then I am wholly committed to them. The God and Father of the Lord Jesus is the God who is concerned for all and at one with all.'

But he could not resist making a side reference to the absurdity of the occasion. Being styled Bishop of Durham and acquiring a territorial signature he said verged on the pretentious and anachronistic.

'We are told that "enthronement" is an ancient symbol of the Bishop's task and privilege to care for and "chair" the diocese. A "throne" is just a chair. Nevertheless, being installed in what is repeatedly claimed to be "the highest throne in Christendom" leaves the representative relationship between a Lord Bishop of Durham and the Lord Jesus Christ inevitably ambiguous . . .

'I face you therefore as an ambiguous, compromised and questioning person, entering on an ambiguous office in an uncertain Church in the midst of a threatened and threatening world. I dare to do this and I even, with fear and trembling, rejoice to do this, because this is where God is to be found. In the midst, that is, of the ambiguities, the compromises, the uncertainties, the questions and the threats of our daily and ordinary worlds. For the Church exists, despite all its failings and all its historically acquired clutter, because the disturbing, provocative, impracticable, loving and utterly God-centred Jesus got himself crucified. Then God vindicated this God-centred way of life, love and being by raising Jesus up.

'So the disillusioned disciples were turned into spirit-filled apostles, and the Church has ever since been learning and re-learning that in the flesh and blood of this man is God's way of being with us, and of giving us a share in the bringing in of his Kingdom. If we long for hope, then we must not fall back on hoping against hope and refusing to face ordinary realities, within us and around us, both in society and in the Church, Nor must we indulge in cheap hope, expecting miracle solutions either from God or from politicians. For we know that keeping hope alive in this sort of a world cost God the cross.

'The cost of hope for us, therefore, is to get rid of all triumphalism and false expectations and to stay with our problems in the power of God and in search of God who

92

is waiting for us and looking for us. If we who are Christians can work this out in the Church and in our religious practices, then we shall also be ready to help to work this out also in society at large and in our community practices. Let me try and explain.

'Because the God who gives himself for us in Jesus Christ and also gives himself to us in the Spirit is so glorious, so gracious and so promising, we Christians are always liable to expect things of him which are contrary to his revealed character and ways of working. God has committed himself to the risk of creation, the identification of incarnation and the perseverance of indwelling. His principal and unique declaration of himself to us is in Jesus, whom we Christians recognize as Christ. There was a glimpse of glory in the Transfiguration, but the fulfilling of the transfiguring glory was the disfiguring of the cross. The resurrection did not avoid rejection, desolation and death. It was brought about through them and out of them. If God goes that way, we can expect no short cuts. We have no right to expect a Church which will guarantee us infallible comfort, a Bible which will assure us of certain truth, charismatic experiences which settle our knowledge of God for good and all, miracles which prove God's presence beyond a doubt, questions which we are quite sure must always be put, or insights into the Kingdom of God which assuredly promise social utopias. We forget again and again that in discovering the resurrection some doubted (Matthew 28:17), at the first Pentecost some asked "What can this mean?" but others said contemptuously, "They have been drinking!" (Acts 2:13), while at the transfiguration Peter was both frightened and confused. God does not impose himself, he gives himself, and our faith, interpretation and obedience are always required to discern him and respond to him.

'Of course we do have the Church to support us, the Bible to judge and renew us, experiences of the Spirit which kindle in us transformation, assurance and joy, miracles

93

which encourage and direct people of faith, questions which we must ask as long as we acknowledge the limitations of the intellect, and a call to relate the Kingdom of God to what is going on in our society. But God must never be identified with his gifts or the occasions of his giving. Above all he does not give us these gifts, of catholicity, of Bible, of charismata, of miracle, of intellect and of social concern for us variously and differently to make party labels of them and to set Catholic against Protestant, against Evangelical, against Charismatic, against Liberal, against Activist. We must be making a mistake about God if we insist that the chief ways in which we personally experience God's gifts and his giving are his only ways or the definitive ways. The greatness, the glory and the freedom of God relativizes all our disputes.

'Christian conflicts, therefore, are not about the *Who*, but about the *How*. Whom we serve is the one and only God known to us through Jesus Christ in the spirit. How we serve is a necessary but secondary matter and whatever the answers in practice and in theory, they are always subordinate to him, and inadequate for him. So none of our ways of understanding God and serving God are, strictly speaking, God's ways. All are our ways which he allows us responsibly and humbly to develop and then submit to his blessing, his judgement, his renewal and, sometimes, his reversal. The cost of hope in renewing the Church, spreading Christian discipleship and growing in Christian unity is the relativizing of us all by the greatness of his glory and by the greatness of the risks which he takes in his love, so that we are set free for new forms of obedience, fresh discoveries of his grace and new ways of working together despite our differences.

'This offer of freedom for newness and hope under the Almightiness of God and through the down-to-earth presence of God is, however, not by any means confined to Christian Churches and religious affairs. There is a power and a possibility here about hope in our present social discontents. Here, again, triumphalism, absolutism and illusions have to be got rid of if we are to find hopeful and human ways forward. The cost of hope in our society and our politics is a responsible readiness for compromise. Once we are clear that nobody has God's view of things or does God's will in God's way, then it also becomes clear that to insist on one's own view and nothing but one's own view and the whole of one's own view, is outrageously self-righteous, deeply inhuman and damnably dangerous. It is to set our inevitable conflicts on course for destructive fights which no one can win, through which all will lose and which could end by destroying us all. Until we reach the Kingdom of God, responsible mutually worked-out compromises will again and again be of the essence both of true godliness and true humility. Anyone who rejects compromise as a matter of policy, programme or conviction is putting himself or herself in the place of God, and Christians and atheists can surely be agreed that, whether there is a God or not, no person or set of persons from our human race is suitable for divine appointment. Consider the bearing of this on our most pressing current social tragedy, the miner's strike.

'It suggests that there must be no victory in the miners' strike. There must be no victory, but a speedy settlement which is a compromise pointing to community and the future. There must be no victory, because the miners must not be defeated. They are desperate for their communities and this desperation forces them to action. No one concerned in this strike, and we are all concerned, must forget for one moment what it is like to be part of a community centred on a mine or a works when that mine or works closes. It is death, depression and desolation. A society which seeks economic progress for material ends must not indifferently exact such human suffering from some for the sake of the affluence of others. The miners then must not be defeated, and this must be the first priority.

'But there must be no victory for them on present terms

because these include negotiation on their terms alone, pits left open at all costs and the endorsement of civil violence for group ends. Yet, equally, there must be no victory for the Government. This Government, whatever it says, seems in action to be determined to defeat the miners and thus treat workers as not part of 'us'. They also seem to be indifferent to poverty and powerlessness. Their financial measures consistently improve the lot of the already better-off while worsening that of the badly-off. Their answer to civil unrest seems to be to make the means of suppression more efficient while ignoring or playing down the causes. Such a government cannot promote community or give hope in the very difficult days we are faced with. It cannot even effectively promote the genuine insights it has about the need for realism in what is economically possible. To wish a victory over the miners is simply to store up trouble not to reduce it.

'And there must be no victory for "us", that is to say society at large in our various groupings, who by our trends, tendencies and voting set up the sort of materialistic and consumer society we have. There will be no new hope for the future if all we get is the end of the strike and therefore, apparently, a quiet life again and the assurances that "they" are dealing with things. Our problems will not go away. We shall find hope only if more and more of us are prepared to face up to what is going on, what is wrong in it, and what might be brought out of it.

'Therefore, a negotiated settlement which is a compromise and demands, of us all, further work on the problems both of the miners and of society at large is the only hopeful thing. But how might this come about? Might it be by Mr MacGregor withdrawing from his chairmanship and Mr Scargill climbing down from his absolute demands? The withdrawal of an imported elderly American to leave a reconciling opportunity for some local product is surely neither dishonourable nor improper. It would show that the interpretation of his appointment as the provocation of the miners to fight in order that they might be defeated was false, and it would indicate that the Government values the cost of hope as much as or more than the fruit of victory. After all, victory leaves hurt and more trouble. Hope has a future. But this would have to be matched by evidence that Mr Scargill too was not an absolutist but a compassionate and realistic negotiator who cares more for people and for the future than for an ideology. Without withdrawal and without climbing down it looks as if we are faced with several people determined to play God. And this gives us all hell.'

And the Bishop concluded, 'We have to face up to what is going on, get involved in what is going on and discern Jesus in what is going on. His gift will be himself, his promise will be the growth of all that is human and his power will be hope. And in the midst of it all our anchor and assurance will be to worship him, to wait for him and to rest in him.'

Bishop Jenkins had put careful and considerable emphasis in his sermon on the doctrines of the incarnation and resurrection without reopening the old theological debate in so many words. His reference to 'triumphalism' and 'absolutism' and 'readiness for compromise' were, however, cleverly two-edged. He was referring to certain elements in the Church as well as certain elements in society.

Reaction to the sermon was swift and predictable, especially from the Conservative parliamentary benches. The Tory M.P. for Wirral South, Barry Porter said, 'I would rather have an imported American who knows something about the industry, than a bishop of the Church of England, who seems to know very little about Christianity. It is beyond me how a bishop at an enthronement can use that occasion to make a political statement on a topic about which he is totally ignorant.'

Another Conservative M.P., the flamboyant Scot, Nicholas Fairbairn, observed, 'His duty is to save souls and not to preach socialism. If he wishes to worship earthly gods like Arthur Scargill, let him forsake the post to which he has been wrongly appointed.' And John Carlisle, Conservative M.P. for Luton North, added for good measure, 'The thunderbolt that struck York Minster might similarly strike Durham.' He also called on the Archbishop of Canterbury to deliver the most severe reprimand in the book.

John Selwyn Gummer M.P., the Party Chairman who is also a member of the Synod, spoke of the sermon's shortcomings.

The reaction to the sermon of the clergy and congregation present in the Cathedral was that of the rare sound of applause. It had been a splendid and majestic service which combined the dignity of years of tradition with a sense of a family occasion. Despite the threat of a boycott by certain clergy a number of prominent evangelicals who might have stayed away decided to attend.

At the beginning of the service, David Jenkins had knocked – as bishops of Durham had done before him – at the cathedral door with his pastoral staff and had been welcomed by the Dean. A cathedral may contain the throne of the bishop but it is the responsibility of the Dean and Chapter. The Bishop took the oaths on the Durham Gospels, the most valuable volume of which was written down by hand in A.D. 700. After his presentation to the people a young family came up from the congregation to present their new bishop with a reminder of the Benedictine history of the Cathedral, a copy of the Rule of St Benedict, a gift from the diocese.

In his word sketch of the day, Michael Sadgrove wrote in the *Church Times*,

It was certainly a remarkable and a brave sermon. Did it go too far? The crowd in the Cathedral made their own response very clear; it was the first time I have heard a sermon spontaneously applauded. There was laughter, too – especially, for instance, when the Bishop acknowledged that he was not everyone's cup of tea.

But the sermon showed beyond doubt that Bishop Jenkins was prepared to be true to the Durham tradition of concerning himself very much with the complex social problems of the North East. And it also showed him to be a man deeply serious about God, about the Incarnation and Resurrection, about the world and his own episcopate.

Such a powerfully God-centred sermon could not but have reassured the people that, theologically, they had little to fear from their new bishop. No doubt he will continue to speak his mind on all sorts of topics as his conscience dictates; and no doubt, too, the diocese of Durham is in for a lively episcopate. But the tone of the service was summoned up by the profound conviction running through the prayers led by the Bishop after his sermon:

'We pray for the world in its need of God. Open our eyes to behold thy glory: make known to us the ways of truth and love; fix our hearts and minds on our Lord and Saviour Jesus Christ.'

From David Jenkins' fellow bishops there was a mixed response to their new colleague's sermon. The Bishop of Peterborough thought that the new bishop had blundered and his first impression was that 'the man had no sense of time or place'. The proper place for a political statement he felt was the House of Lords. The Archbishop of York did not think it inappropriate for a bishop starting his ministry in a mining community to refer to the strike. But he added a qualification, 'I am not sure that it was wise to criticize individuals by name in a sermon, but this is a caution I would apply to any sermon in any circumstances and not just to this one.'

It was the reference to Mr MacGregor by name rather than the general thrust of his foray into matters political which attracted the attention and the criticism. Only a week before, when preaching in Derby Cathedral prior to visiting the mining community of Creswell, the Archbishop of Canterbury had warned of the 'bitter harvest' the dispute would bring. The Creswell pit was working but had been the site of some very ugly scenes as striking miners attempted to picket it. Dr Runcie said that the seeds of anger and mistrust had already taken root, and continued:

'I appeal to every Christian involved in the mining industry, whether directly or indirectly, whether in management or union or among the rank-and-file, to work together to consider how a new spirit of peace-making, how a willingness to go the extra mile, can begin to work its way into our angry and divided communities and draw the poison out of bitter words.'

While Dr Runcie's and David Jenkins' messages had run in parallel, the way their contributions had been reported contrasted sharply. The Archbishop had studiously avoided references to personalities in either camp which could in any way be construed as derogatory.

There was something of a storm in a tea cup however when the Archbishop was discovered to have written to Mr MacGregor in his own hand, regretting any personal hurt the Bishop's remarks might have caused him. Did the letter amount to an official apology? Lambeth said no. The Archbishop, it was said, supported the general tone of David Jenkins' sermon but had sympathized with the Coal Board Chairman for any hurt the remarks may have caused him or his family. He had written the letter as a pastoral act in the spirit of reconciliation advocated by David Jenkins. 'It was a letter', Dr Runcie said, 'between two Christians. I wanted to use it as a personal example of the reconciliation we are all trying to preach about and talk about.'

The affair was neatly encapsulated in a *Guardian* leader of 28 September. It was headed 'A Note in Edgeways'.

The Archbishops of Durham and Canterbury [*sic.*], and Mr Ian MacGregor, are embroiled in much ado about very little. Durham made a thoughtful and ritually balanced speech which tried to say that the striking miners should not be 'beaten' like Argentine soldiers on Mount Tumbledown. A profusion of media commentators chose to see this as an amazing attack on Mrs Thatcher's 'victory' prospects (though that was only half of the message). Dr Runcie, berated yet again for leading 'the S.D.P. at prayer', defended Durham's 'robust' message. But privately, being a nice chap, he thought Dr Jenkins' characterization of Mr MacGregor as an 'elderly, imported American' a little cheap. Mr MacGregor is, of course, 72, on contract from Wall Street, and a Florida voter. But even so (presumably because they might sometimes sip sherry together at some functions) Canterbury dropped a personal little note to MacGregor hoping the touch of polemic hadn't gone amiss. The Coal Board Chairman dropped a personal little note back. Then there was a leak and much ado. Dr Runcie behaved throughout like a normal, caring, decent human being in perfectly comprehensible circumstances. There are many, many issues at stake in the pit dispute. This isn't one of them.

Yet, although the Bishop can be criticized for introducing a distracting personal reference into his sermon, it cannot be denied that his intervention in the debate proved to be the catalyst to a comprehensive discussion of the many issues at stake. The issues had by that point in the dispute become overshadowed by the personalities and politics involved. David Jenkins, if nothing else, provoked the Secretary of State, Peter Walker, to restate the Government's basic case for a rationalization of the coal industry and the appointment of Mr MacGregor to do the job. The Government at the time seemed to prefer resting its public relations strategy on the public's emotional reaction to the television pictures of picket-line violence and tales of persecuted working miners.

Mr Walker, known as the last 'wet' in the Cabinet, had given an immediate thought on the Bishop's sermon in a speech to his Worcester constituents at the weekend following the enthronement. Despite his reputation for being the least doctrinaire or dogmatic Conservative, thereby earning the description invented by the Prime Minister of 'wet', his first words were full of typical party rhetoric. He attacked Bishop Jenkins for preaching sermons about 'fiction rather than facts'. The prelate, he suggested, might like to say 'a few prayers' for working miners who for months had been suffering misery at the hands of the mobs.

However, the Secretary for Energy decided not just to address the faithful party members behind the Bishop's back but also to write to the Bishop putting a more reasoned case. He began by outlining what he had achieved on behalf of the mining communities, and continued:

> You have preached that the miners must not be 'defeated'. But you have not clarified who is trying to defeat them. You imply that it is Mr MacGregor and the Government. Such an implication has no justification whatsoever.
>
> We have never tried to defeat the miners. We have tried to see that they were victorious to a degree unsurpassed in the history of the mining industry. We tried to give them a guarantee of a better life, devoid of any industrial strike or unrest.
>
> Please examine, as a Christian bishop, the sequence of events which occurred before Mr Scargill decided for the first time in your lifetime to call a national strike in his industry without giving his members the right of a ballot.

Mr Walker then gave a run-through of the money the

government had invested in the industry and the employment guarantees it had given to miners, and continued:

As a Christian I hope that in your moments of meditation and prayer you will ask why the 70,000 miners who were given a democratic vote decided overwhelmingly not to strike.

At such moments you could also ponder why it is that these men have day after day been threatened by mobs from outside their own communities. Mobs which have used violence and intimidation in order to prevent men who follow the normal traditions of the N.U.M from acting in accordance with the position of the majority of their colleagues.

In your sermon you stated 'that there must be no victory for the miners on present terms because this would mean pits left open at all costs and the endorsement of civil violence for group ends'. I do hope you recognize that this phrase explains the reason why miners have suffered so much for so long.

During this entire dispute Mr Scargill has not been interested in discussing the wages, the guarantee of no compulsory redundancies, the investment in the future or the offers prepared to assist mining communities.

He has only made one demand and has only been willing to discuss one factor. This is the demand that any pit, no matter how uneconomic, should be kept open until the last tonne of coal is exhausted or until safety prevents the continuation of operations.

No miners' leader has ever made such a demand. No Government and no National Coal Board management has ever or could ever concede such a demand. Mr Scargill has never moved or negotiated upon it. . . .

Perhaps neither you nor I can analyse accurately his motives. But, if you have embarked upon a study of Mr Scargill's written and spoken words over many years, you can only come to the conclusion that he has always favoured conflict as opposed to participation, because he believes it is by conflict with the existing system that his utopia will be achieved.

Having stated in your sermon that you feel the necessity for Mr Scargill and the miners to move from this demand, can I perhaps ask you as a Christian bishop what you believe the Government or the nation should do if Mr Scargill continues, as he has for six months, to refuse to negotiate or to move from this demand? . . .

I cannot judge the degree to which I have succeeded in getting the balance correct on this particular issue. I do know that in my moments of meditation and prayer I have genuinely attempted to the best of my ability to understand the hopes and aspirations of miners and their communities. I have persuaded my Cabinet colleagues to devote considerable economic resources to see that their reasonable aspirations can be satisfied.

If I had considered that Mr MacGregor was a man who had either been instructed or personally had the intention of destroying the mining industry, or that he was contemptuous of miners or their communities, I would of course have dismissed him immediately. . . .

Perhaps your observations on Mr MacGregor were based upon his image as portrayed in propaganda rather than upon the genuine aspirations or faults of the man himself.

You and I agree that the miners must not be defeated. But we must do our best to assess who is the true enemy.

Peter Walker.

The letter from the Minister was not one which could go unanswered. It was an invitation to take part in a public exchange of correspondence, and on 28 September David Jenkins wrote his reply from Auckland Castle. He thanked Mr Walker for his 'reasoned and informative' letter and said that he greatly appreciated 'both the courtesy and the compassion' expressed. . . .

Unfortunately, the government to which you belong does not seem to care for the steadily increasing number of people who are unemployed, and are otherwise marginalized in society, and does not seem to care that it does not seem to care.

On all the statistical tables known to me it seems a simple matter of fact that this government's fiscal measures consistently improve the lot of (to use titles from one such table) 'senior managers' and 'company directors' while causing losses to 'jobless man with family' and 'semi-skilled worker'. This seems a gratuitous refusal to care and a rather insulting determination to make sure that the already under-privileged bear an even greater share of the cost of our undoubted economic difficulties, and of our undoubtedly required greater economic realism. It is also difficult to believe that the government does care for all the members of our society when cuts are repeatedly made on those services which are of particular value to the poor, but money can always be found for military adventures in the Falklands, pretending to be still a great power in defence matters or keeping up the police forces. I do not say that we can do without either defence or police expenditure, but the emphasis does seem to be persistently on non-caring and aggressive directions.

This leads to the second principal point. I agree with you that Mr Scargill's personal intransigence has played and does play a very considerable part in keeping the situation over the mines deadlocked. . . . But it is necessary to ask why Mr Scargill gets the (by no means complete, but very strong) support that he does. . . . Redundancy payments are all very well, and the redundancy arrangements of the N.C.B. may well be the envy of threatened workers elsewhere, but redundancy means both no further jobs for the redundant, and no jobs for their children. Communities and a whole way of life are swept away at a time when there are no alternatives elsewhere. This is a vital difference between closing mines in the 1960s and early 1970s and closing them now. . . .

Then, on the other hand, Mr Scargill's intransigence is immensely reinforced by a government style which seems to make a virtue of confrontation. I had hoped, when I first drafted my enthronement sermon two or three weeks before the event, that the page on the miners' strike could be either withdrawn or completely rewritten. But the Prime Minister's remarks on 'The Jimmy Young Programme' reported in the papers of September 20th, convinced me that, with great sadness and perplexity, I could not alter a word. We seem to have intransigence confronted by intransigence, and this, I believe, is the death both of true politics and true community. . . .

If the government is really prepared to contemplate the pit strike going on for more than a year, then it seems to me to have lost all sense of what a community is and what a country is. Something must be done speedily to stop communities tearing themselves apart, to stop bully boys in both mining pickets and police forces calling the tune, to stop the mining industry destroying itself. . . .

If the strike continues, it is certain that miners, government and country will have been defeated. It is therefore, surely, in the last analysis, up to the government to consider what concession it can possibly make to break this dreadfully threatening deadlock, and free us all for further chances to tackle our problems without confrontation politics at every turn.

As you say, 'We must do our best to assess who is the true enemy.' I think that Christian insight would encourage us to recognize that *part* of the enemy is always within ourselves, and that no 'they', 'he' or 'she' should ever be treated as the total enemy, and the sole enemy. This does not make for simplicity of party slogans. But I think it does make for a compassion which if exercised politically might greatly add to efficiency and hope.

And David Jenkins signed the letter with his new epis-copal and territorial signature, David Dunelm, using as is traditional the old Latin word for the city of Durham.

A second volley of letters followed, but they were shorter and even blunter, and followed a private face-to-face meeting between the two men. Mr Walker challenged the Bishop to tell the public his views on Arthur Scargill. 'I know you have made a considerable study of Marxist theory and practice ... where do you think he fits into all this?' The Energy Secretary pointed the Bishop to Mr Scargill's own words in the *New Left Review* when he had written about his 'mob successes' at Saltley Coke Works in 1972. 'Here', Mr Scargill had written, 'was the living proof that the working class had only to flex its muscles and it could bring governments, employers, society, to a total standstill.'

Mr Walker challenged the Bishop to give his opinion. He asked, 'Do you feel the writings, oratory and actions of Mr Scargill are just those of somebody displaying a degree of personal intransigence? Or do you feel they are the actions of somebody on a political crusade which is contrary to the desires of the majority of the people in our country?'

Mr Walker then turned to the question of Mr Scargill and mass picketing. 'I must ask you as a Christian bishop, why does he ignore T.U.C. guidelines, and his own union, that only six peaceful pickets can operate at a colliery entrance? Why have there been 7,000 arrests on criminal charges? Why have there been victimizations and beatings up on a massive scale? Why has Mr Scargill never on any occasion appealed for violence by the picket mobs to stop?'

David Jenkins' reply sent from Bishop Auckland on 9 October illustrated how the two men, bishop and minister, were talking at cross purposes. Mr Walker wanted to pin the bishop down to condemn the shortcomings of the National Union of Mineworkers, their approach and the motives of the leadership. The Bishop again wanted to see the dispute in the wider context of the impact of government policy on the nation. He wrote:

Dear Mr Walker

You keep asking me to 'look at the facts', by which you mean the details of particular government programmes and the Coal Board offers. I keep asking you (and the whole government and the country at large) also to 'look at the facts', by which I mean broader impressions, aspirations, and trends which provide the context, and the pressures within which these programmes, and these offers, are perceived and received. Unless we can converse about the interaction of these two levels we shall be trapped in a dialogue of the deaf, instead of developing realistic discussions about ways forward in a world which includes miners caught in bewildered and divided communities, militant Marxists exploiting other people's confusions and a confused and divided country faced by a deadlock which daily threatens more violence and a winter of discontent greater than any we have yet experienced.

The impressions include that of a government which cares more for a particular line in economic policy than for those who have to bear the costs of that policy: the aspirations include a desire to be recognized and acknowledged as rightly longing for continuing communities and a continuing place in the working world; and the trends include a steady experience for the poor of getting poorer, and having less services available to them. Maybe no present government could avoid much of this, but that makes it all the more essential that any government clearly recognizes and responds to all of this. They must show that they include the burdened, the excluded, and those who find themselves with less and less share of what cake there is, in their current practical understanding of society, and their assessment of the costs and of future programmes.

Unless this point is taken I do not see how we can usefully discuss 'the Scargill phenomenon'. Why does he get away with it? I deplore his refusal to organize a ballot, and his readiness to organize intimidation which breaks out into wider violence. I also reject his apparent attachment to a Stalinist type of Marxism which is thoroughly discredited both in theory and in practice. I would, of course, be obliged to resist his desire, if it became part of practical politics, to model the government of this country on current Eastern European models. But I do not believe he is as clever as Lenin, and I do not believe that the working classes of this country are ripe for a revolution organized by a Bolshevik-type minority. There would not be even a glimmer of a suggestion that they were, if many of them were not feeling themselves pushed into helplessness and hopelessness – and, above all, that they were being ignored.

A Christian bishop is bound not only to deplore violence but also to press searching questions about the distribution of the causes of violence. A Christian bishop is bound to risk the appearance of bias in drawing attention to the cause for those who get the least from society or the least chance to contribute to society. A Christian bishop is bound to make a nuisance of himself to those in authority by troubling them with the suggestion that because their power is great they may well have to make the concession, or accept the partial but temporary defeat, which will enable a new alignment of forces and a fresh attempt at working together at our problems. It is neither unrealistic nor sentimental to suggest that intransigent opponents may best be undermined by a readiness to compromise, and to accept partially unsatisfactory solutions for the sake of building wider alliances and mitigating well established suspicions and fears.

To go forward we need to get down to the wider considerations which the Bishop of Birmingham and the Archbishop of Canterbury have recently raised, and we also need to get on with intensive negotiations out of the public eye. It would presumably be best to let our public correspondence rest at any rate for the time being?

The concluding paragraph referred to the interview given to *The Times* by the Archbishop and the address of Bishop Montefiore to the Birmingham Diocesan Synod. Bishop Montefiore, while criticizing the union leadership for condoning violence and refusing to honour the democratic process, had attacked the government's 'politics of confrontation'. Dr Runcie had challenged the whole government economic policy which led, he claimed, to unemployment, poverty and despair. He had denounced inequitable sacrifice and those who 'treat people as scum'.

In the theological debate David Jenkins was perceived by the public as a maverick, although in fact he held views very much in line with a wide body of established liberal opinion. So it was in the realm of politics. While his views might have been construed as left-wing and anti-government, they were entirely in step with the consensus of opinion on the bench of bishops. The Bishop of Birmingham had spoken of the fear that motivated the miners, 'fear for the future of their children and whole communities', and 'a fear of becoming powerless in a land where those in power don't seem to care'.

In his new home, the north-east, David Jenkins was making a special point of identifying himself with the hard-pressed and fearful communities in his charge. On 28 September he preached at the pit village of South Hetton to mark the 140th anniversary of the Haswell Colliery explosion, in which ninety-five men had died. His theme was the need for communities to keep going in the face of disasters; he said how important it was for the Church to help overcome the sense of helplessness felt by many people today.

David Jenkins' readiness to identify himself and the Church with a political stance should not have come as a surprise. Neither should the immediate willingness of his Church to back him have been unexpected. Writing in *The Times* on 25 September, the paper's Religious Affairs Correspondent, Clifford Longley, wrote perceptively:

> The whole mood of the Church at present is coldly hostile to Mrs Thatcher and her Ministers, and there is not much affection in the other direction.
>
> The situation was ripe, therefore, for someone a little more outspoken than the average churchman to say what most of them feel . . . it had to be the Bishop of Durham who gave expression to the Church's unease.

The Church, Mr Longley wrote, is committed to the middle way both theologically and politically. When consensus politics were abandoned in 1979, with the extremes of Left and Right taking the dominant role in British politics, it became increasingly difficult to remain non-political, as to hold the middle view could appear to favour one side or other in the political row.

Clifford Longley then pointed to another issue going deeper than a clash of political temperament.

> Mrs Thatcher has said on several occasions that one of the primary aims of her political life was to bring about a 'moral revolution' in society: in other words, to alter basic ethical values . . . and this touches the Church on a very raw nerve. It understands itself, not the Government, as being the guardian of private and public morality, the spiritual arm of the state . . .
>
> The case is not, as cynics would say, that the Established Church is looking for something useful and important to do, having lost ground as it has lost members. It is that societies fall inevitably into deeper and deeper conflict unless there is some general agreement about the moral ground-rules. Thus marriages will collapse, unless there is general agreement that adultery

is wrong; and industrial relations will collapse, unless there is general agreement in favour of give-and-take negotiated settlements . . .

The Bishop of Durham, in fact, goes one step further along the argument than this. The same sermon which attacked the Government contained an extremely blunt analysis of the Church of England's own standing in society. He seemed to be asking himself whether he really was 'Bishop of Durham' in the old establishment sense, or whether he was just a leader of one, not tremendously significant, religious group in that society.

Such thoughts suggest that the Church of England is some way off from being able to lead the nation toward a moral consensus. In that case it makes sense, not to stand above the rough and tumble of political argument, but charge right into the middle of it.

12

Read, Marx, learn . . .

In 1976 the S.C.M. Press published a book by David Jenkins entitled *The Contradiction of Christianity*. The book evolved from a series of Edward Cadbury Lectures delivered at Birmingham University two years before, and the 'contradiction' of the title referred to that between the ideals of the Gospel message and the record of behaviour of Christians and Christian institutions. God is to be seen in the contradiction, David Jenkins argued, without its being resolved.

The book was also very much involved with a study of Marx. Call contradiction 'dialectic', and Marxism is where one arrives. David Jenkins was not one to shun Marxism on dogmatic grounds; 'It would be a betrayal of the Christian faith to be afraid of collaboration with Marxists where the particular oppression of a political situation and the particular aims of a short- or medium-term strategy required it.'

If more senior Conservatives had been familiar with the work they might not have been so surprised to hear the Bishop addressing immediate political issues in his enthronement sermon.

The book starts with an examination of what David Jenkins describes as the tribalism of Christian traditions.

Christian tribalism . . . demonstrates condescension, arrogance and indifference to 'lesser breeds without the law', it is necessarily related to identity, and it is exer-

113

cised in dehumanizing ways . . . 'Me and my group' in our self-understanding are held to be the universal norm of both humanity and salvation. The attitudes and behaviour which follow from this are both dehumanizing and destructive of the very message of salvation from which the original identity was drawn.

The critical question to be asked by all Christians, therefore, is whether Marx was right in suggesting that Christianity is nothing but an ideology emanating from specific social and historical structures. Or are many Third-World Christians right when they argue that the value of Marx lies only in his serving to draw our attention to the ideological, cultural and 'tribal conditioning' of expressions of Christianity.

If these conditionings are recognised for what they are, then liberation can be received so that the message of the gift of God and of the infinite possibilities of man once more emerges to be a human gospel indeed.

It is my understanding that this latter possibility exists because of the reality of Transcendence in the midst, of the presence and action of the God who again and again overthrows the limitations of both individual and social human pathology and who is, mercifully, too much for both the tribalisms of Christianity and the determinism of Marxism.

The lessons to be learned from Marx, says David Jenkins, include acquiring an

understanding that social reality involves exploitation, conflict and a control over the production of ideas, including our ideas of what is real, just and appropriate to various classes of human.

Do we therefore conclude that the total cause of man's inhumanity to man is oppression (distorting both

114

oppressors and oppressed and accounting for all their various malformations of themselves and of one another) and that the only obstacle to being and becoming human is constituted by the social structures of class and exploitation with their roots in economic power? And so do we further hold that our hopes for what is involved in being and becoming human lie in the class struggle now and the emergence, via the dictatorship of the proletariat, of the classless society?

The diagnosis of Marxism has to be taken absolutely seriously while the claim to absoluteness – of diagnosis, of description and of hope – has to be rejected. To locate the cause of man's contradictions of himself solely in oppression and the obstacles to overcoming these contradictions in social and economic structures seems to be a dangerously insufficient account of what is involved both in the human dilemma and in the human possibility, while the hope and assurance of a future solution and resolution through the class struggle to a classless society seems to be quite unrealistic and groundless.

There could have been no more unequivocal assurance to Mr Walker and the Conservatives that the Bishop was not ideologically hand-in-glove with Mr Scargill. However, it did not mean that there were not times when Christians and Marxists might tread the same path.

The Marxist criticism of our society converges at some important points with the biblical and prophetic judgement which is proclaimed upon the treatment of the poor and the excluded. . . . Christians who become aware of the extent of the identification of the Church with the privileged *status quo* suffer a strong sense of guilt and of shock. They are moved and disturbed . . . The Marxist analysis reinforces the condemnation which these awakened Christians feel that they and their Church both need and deserve, while at the same time a positive way

115

forward is indicated. . . . Many Christians who turn to Marxism are excited by the way in which men and women among the poor and the oppressed discover themselves and find hope in being themselves as they begin to take on their historical role according to this doctrine and analysis. If you discover that you can organise and work together to achieve something for yourself then you also discover that you are indeed a self. And this discovery can be made through and in the solidarity and purposiveness of the struggle whether or not the struggle leads to immediate achievement. Thus Christians have come to see this discovery by the poor and oppressed that they can have a part, a meaning, and a hope in the shaping of their own lives, as real foretastes or sacraments of the Kingdom of God.

Although David Jenkins was writing some eight years before the events of the miners' strike, it was in many ways prophetic. Many Christians who lived and worked in the pit communities took a full part in the organization of life during the dispute. The villages, and those in the northeast were no exception, developed a camaraderie and comradeship and network of self-help groups to sustain life during the months of hardship. For month after month households received little or no money. Families had their meals at communal soup kitchens; televisions and cars were sold, children went without presents at birthdays and Christmas, and yet there is much evidence to suggest that the morale of the communities was often never higher. Neighbours met and spoke and co-operated; people became less selfish and self-centred.

David Jenkins argues that, as important as Marxism is, there is an important ingredient missing.

. . . it is a desperate myth, for it points only to something no living person will enjoy and it hopes for a historical

116

reality which must contradict all the contradictions of history.

For the Christian, the theory and practice of man in the image of God is complemented by the experience and hope of the power and the future of the Kingdom of God.

The basis, the energy and the fulfilment of all relationships is love. This is so because God is love and God is the basis, the energy and the fulfilment of things. . . .

The ultimate future and fulfilment of being human lies neither in revolution nor extinction but in transfiguration.

In October 1984 the journal *Marxism Today* published an interview with the Bishop of Durham. An unusual publication in which to find a bishop, and no doubt an article about a bishop was an unusual occurrence for the magazine. He was interviewed by Andrew Heywood who explored in lay language the areas where the two creeds, Christianity and Marxism, could co-operate and where they inevitably diverged.

DAVID JENKINS: . . . the Church, in my view rightly, is involved in political and social affairs, it does have to keep on thinking very hard about its distinctive role and not simply jump on any particular bandwagon. . . . It ought to be witnessing to the transcendence of God and the involvement of God in the world and, therefore, ought to be able to pay attention to questions and difficulties of its people and opponents.

The Church will always, as far as I can see, be in an ambiguous position. The principal role of the Church is twofold. First, to keep on pointing to the judgement of God – so it ought to be a disturbing influence. Secondly, to be as understanding and as sympathetic as possible of all the different positions people take with regard both to this judgement and to political problems.

On the whole the Church of England has preferred to

be content with the ambiguous position and has not been a sufficiently disturbing element. It ought to be more of a disturber, constantly drawing attention, for example, to the obscenity of nuclear weapons and having nothing to do with any suggestion that it could be morally right. It may be politically inevitable but you have to get out of the inevitability as soon as you can. Equally it should be drawing attention to the way in which, if you go for nothing but the profit motive, then you are betraying your love for your neighbour. How you work it out is another question and Christians, like anyone else, can't necessarily agree about that.

ANDREW HEYWOOD: You were previously Director of Humanum Studies at the World Council of Churches. How do you think the Church of England has responded to the radical efforts of the W.C.C. in such areas as racialism, Latin America and apartheid?

DAVID JENKINS: It has actually responded almost more than we might have hoped for. I think that the climate of opinion about many of the World Council of Churches' initiatives has steadily changed over the years. That has to be set against the conservative reaction we are talking about, but, on the other hand, there is much more discussion of these more radical ideas in places like the deanery synods.

The main point we've got to tackle is that people suppose, if you are being Christian, that you will somehow be soothing and comforting in a bland sense. It is quite clear to me from the Bible that you are up against this battle between good and evil all the time. We have got to get people to see that the job of the Church is to strengthen people for the battle and in the battle, and to see that there is always more than just the battle. To put it another way, we are not determined by the class conflict, but the class conflict is a real thing and so how do we live in relation to it? . . .

ANDREW HEYWOOD: The Church in Britain has never had to respond to a strong Marxist party whereas the Roman Church, in particular, has entered into dialogue with Marxist governments, has encouraged strong Marxist presence within its own membership and has engaged in revolutionary struggle in Latin America. What do you feel about the coexistence of Marxism with a Christian Church?

DAVID JENKINS: From my experience at the World Council of Churches I think it is a matter of pragmatic political situations. When you have extreme right-wing exploitative minorities, as in Latin America, it is quite clear that the only response, on behalf of people at large, must be to fight such a regime. Christians draw their inspiration from their established gospel and there are Christian Marxists, Marxist Christians and Marxists who draw their inspiration from elsewhere. The matter is one for pragmatics – joining together to fight blatant injustice. But, of course, once you have overthrown the regime the political conflicts are liable to return around those Marxists who seem to be more of the Stalinist type and who invest their hope in Marxism in a total way and those Marxists who are much more humanist Marxists and are therefore pragmatic after the revolution as well as before.

There is undoubtedly a fundamental clash between Christianity and Marxism. On one line of interpretation Marxism is a total explanation of everything and, of course, Christians cannot have that. Although they too have been dogmatic in their time. So there is always likely to be a clash. But many, as I do, believe in the political necessity of taking up with Marxism insofar as certain Marxist analyses on certain points are the best guidance forward But attempt to absolutise Marxism and the battle starts again . . .

ANDREW HEYWOOD: You point to the probability of distortion in Marxism. You have also written that Christians can, at least, hope that God would smash their trivialities and distortions. Given the historical development of Christianity can you see this as a valid claim?

DAVID JENKINS: Well, yes, because it looks to me as though one of the features of Christian history is the capacity to keep on generating reforming self-criticism or to be reminded that there are things which they have forgotten and which they had better come back to. One cannot probabilitize this or guarantee it. One's theoretical stance, whether Christian or Marxist, is an act of faith – not a scientific thing. And what I am bothered about is finding people who are open to be judged themselves in relation both to their ideas and their aims. Although Marxism has gone wrong and, I think, there are a good many things in Marxism which look like being wrong in principle, Christianity too has gone terribly wrong. So I cannot rule out on ethical or ideological grounds the collaboration of Christians and Marxists under given political circumstances for clear human aims. It has not come up as sharply in this country as elsewhere. But, although the polarisation which is developing will not come about in the form of Russia in 1917 nor in Latin America today, the issues that are raised by Marxism are going to have to be faced.

ANDREW HEYWOOD: One section of society which does seem to have faced up to it and which has brought a fresh approach to problems of society and our political response is women. The dynamism of the women's movement has forced a male-dominant society to rethink some of its approach. Apart from the basic issues of ordination and theological tradition, where is the Church on this question of women in society?

DAVID JENKINS: The Church, like the rest of society is only beginning to wrestle with this and a whole lot of people are refusing to face it. The Church is in a muddle, but it does have the positive side which is where discerning voices in the Church should say that one of the hopeful things in our present trouble is very often this disturbing element. It does not mean that they are always right but it does mean that here is something of fundamental creative importance. In the ethnic minorities too, although being black does not make a person right any more than being white does, their pressure is making a disturbing positive element. I would have thought that the Church ought to develop a notion of God the disturber and say 'of course we shall be disturbed'. I am moved by women's liberation and by ethnic groups. But they can be positively received. They must not be idolised. There are no immediate solutions but there are new breakthrough points. . . .

ANDREW HEYWOOD: Your whole operation rests on faith and your conduct relates to a sense of obedience to God as you understand it. Yet, to pick up another depressing issue of the present – young people who have no hope and no future to look to – these people do not understand what it is to have a faith in God, never mind guidance of the Holy Spirit. How are you going to talk to them?

DAVID JENKINS: I think that is the greatest challenge there is. I hope to be part of the Church getting to grips with the sort of things we have been talking about and finding some worthwhile things to do together with people who live in these depressing situations. Until you find worthwhile things to do you cannot entertain the notion of hope, or love, or neighbourliness and so there is no point in going on to talk about God in that situation. In the end it will be a question of stimulating groups of people to live in these situations in such a way as to rekindle community around something to do and something to fight for. The fighting element is going to be there – that is why we are going to go on having a conflict. One of the great challenges is for people who are not so underprivileged to respond to this conflict in a way which will be positive and not to treat it as just a symptom to be dealt with. . . .

People have concentrated more and more on appropriate individual spirituality, appropriate reforms in worship, problems of undertstanding the Bible in an intellectual way, but have forgotten what in one sense was the positive side of Christendom – to think about the whole world and to be concerned about it. So the whole business of what you might call learning and developing practical Christian social ethics has been a very low priority.

In the context of the Third World that business has involved the evolution of liberation theology, which has in turn brought the radical clergy into conflict with right-wing government and the Vatican. In the 1985 Hibbert Lecture the Bishop of Durham attempted to fashion a liberation theology for the affluent part of the world.

> We need to rediscover that we were not mistaken when we committed ourselves, with a considerable degree of consensus, to working out a Welfare State which would substantially contribute to setting people free from unnecessary ill-health, hopeless poverty or acute want and which would make some movement, however slight, along the path to more justice, more caring and less thoughtless and ignored exploitation. . . .
>
> What essays in various aspects and forms of liberation theology would do is to remind those of us who are Christians that God has an investment in the human project and that we are called to collaborate with him in furthering this project . . .
>
> British essays in liberation theology would not be mere echoes or reflections of liberation theology elsewhere. As I learnt from my contacts with some of those who developed liberation theology in Latin America and South East Asia, it would not be in the spirit of liberation theology if they were. As an article published in the

Philippines in Manila in 1971 puts it, 'The question is not "how can we adapt theology to our needs?" rather, how can our needs create a theology which is our own?' Liberation theology rises out of the particular needs of a particular country for hope in relation to justice, peace and love . . . .

To give up the central concerns of the Welfare State and the Beveridge Report because we have run into difficulties is sheer faithlessness and inhumanity. To return to the ethos of 19th-century entrepreneurial individualism is either nostalgic nonsense or else a firm declaration that individual selfishness and organised greed are the only effective motivations for human behaviour. Of course we must be realistic about sin. Romantic utopianism which supposes that all will be well both with the needs of production and with the way power is exercised once 'the people are set free' to be in charge of their own common possessions and their own common destiny, makes the disastrous mistake of rooting all human failings in our social and economic structures, and ignores the role of our often selfish and grasping heads and hearts and spirits. But to promote a materialistic market-orientated individualism as the key to human and social progress is to make an equally destructive mistake about the possibilities and needs of men and women and to turn one's back on real political and social progress which has been made. Realism about sin should not lead to cynicism about altruism and justice, or pessimism about the possibilities of collective organisation and communal caring. In the name of the God of the Bible and of Jesus Christ we must challenge all this and look for renewed ways forward . . .

Secondly, we must insist on the urgent reality and relevance of the judgement of God. To ignore the poor or to claim that they cannot be counted into society until we have made more money or that we must lay greater burdens on them to ensure that they are more ready to work at any cost is morally questionable, prudentially dangeous (for how much pressure will how many take for how long?) and a deliberate declaration of no sympathy or compassion with their plight. A society which does such things deliberately and refuses to recognise that that is what it is doing, is a society which is tearing itself apart and heading for turbulence and disaster . . . . To progress we shall need all our personal and communal resources as well as all our economic ones, every effort has to be made to combat attitudes, events and statistics which suggest that the substantial minority of our fellows are second or third class citizens or not even citizens at all. To recognise that our society is under judgement for what it is doing to the steadily increasing number of those who are excluded from the benefits enjoyed by the majority, is not to know at once what is to be done about them. It is however to recognise them as citizens along with us to commit ourselves to conscious, explicit and shared efforts to develop our common good and multiply our common resources. It is also to acknowledge the urgency of this judgement and to challenge the complacent enjoyment of jam today by some, when for others there is no promise even of jam tomorrow.

Thirdly, a liberation theology will search for ways of innovation, experiment and risk . . . Many unthinkable things (e.g. maximum and minimum wages) will have to become thinkable, including, probably, government risks over decentralisation and regionalisation.

Fourthly and finally, liberation theology will have to work at building up communities of endurance around a celebration of the gospel of the God who is committed to our world, our society and our future for the sake of His Kingdom. For it is certain that we shall have much to endure, including uncertainty, turbulence, violence and people feeling that there is no hope and no way forward.

'They don't seem to care'

While representing a commonly held position on the liberal wing of the Church, David Jenkins' analysis of Marx and its relevance to Christianity is not universally shared.

There was a tendency in particular for those who opposed David Jenkins' theological opinions to disagree with him politically as well. The most notable critic to take issue on both fronts was the man one senior to him in the Church hierarchy, the Bishop of London, the Right Reverend Graham Leonard.

In his preface to the booklet by Dr Murray Harris, *Easter in Durham, Bishop Jenkins and the Resurrection of Jesus*, the Bishop of London wrote,

> to see the Resurrection as no more than a spiritual experience is to abandon the biblical view and to pronounce a decree absolute between spirit and matter. Such an attitude conflicts both with the biblical teaching and, being based on an outdated positivism, with the scientific understanding of man as a psychosomatic unity. The deep and rich objective mystery of re-creation in Christ, which calls for the fullest exercise of all our faculties if we are to be grasped by its meaning, is replaced by a bloodless and subjective experience.

Without mentioning him by name, the Bishop of London, when writing in the *Mail on Sunday* on 14 October 1984, was equally firm in his view that his brother at Durham should not have become so deeply involved in the miners' strike.

Forty years ago, when the Church was involved in a similar secular controversy, one exasperated critic said: 'Politics are the concern of Downing Street, not Canterbury.'

Now that is an extreme view which I have little sympathy with since I believe it is the right and duty of the Christian Church to concern itself with every sphere of human activity. But it is not the role of the Church to govern.

One of the things we should be doing in such difficult times is to encourage responsibility at all levels. But how can we achieve this by seeking to take away from Government its responsibility by trying to do its job?

What are in danger of becoming blurred if we claim an expertise in politics, industry or economics which we do not have, are the very real differences between good and evil, love and hate, justice and injustice.

Three days earlier in *The Daily Telegraph* Dr Edward Norman, the Dean of Peterhouse, Cambridge, had addressed himself to the same issue, the Church and the miners' strike, but some of what he wrote has more in common with the Bishop of London's theological criticism.

For however good their intentions, and however properly they may have attuned their yearning for social righteousness, the fact is that contemporary Church leaders frequently fail to appreciate the real nature of their own spiritual function. They have, indeed, succumbed to a material view of man and his purpose in the world. The real danger of mankind, in this and in every age – but perhaps peculiarly in this, because of the prevalence of non-religious ideologies – derives from threats not to his material but to his spiritual condition.

126

The duties of a priesthood relate precisely to that priority; the Church exists to declare and nurture the spiritual capacity of each person. The material condition of each, to which every age so easily gives a worldly priority, is a very secondary consideration and may anyway be left to those accomplished in the things of the world. The ordinary sense of human decency, the benevolent principle which in ancient cultures was regarded as simply part of the natural law – as something which defined a civilised man from a barbarian – has now been elevated within Christianity as if it is not only specifically Christian but is actually the central point of reference of all religious awareness.

Christianity is being defined in terms of only one of its components – its ethical element – because that is the characteristic it shares with the common assumptions of all decent people. This has the advantage of pleasing the secular moralists, of giving the clergy the impression that they are still fulfilling a 'relevant' social role, and of accommodating the Church to the world in a way that seems challenging and compassionate. But the ethical element as now understood within the Church is deeply materialistic: it is concerned with social benefits and with easing the lot of mankind.

The whole tenor of social development within the modern world has emphasised human security. This is not just because it is comfortable for mankind to have his material existence wrapped in protective coverings, it is contended: it is also claimed as no less a human right. All the benefits of welfare legislation, the impulses of social justice that issue in economic redistribution, and the apparently ceaseless endeavours to domesticate the physical environment, are signs of human attempts to make life painless and safe; and whatever good consequences may accrue, for mankind in general they are having the effect of hauling down a thick curtain of materialism.

When Church leaders identify the application of their faith with exactly the same sorts of cosmic attempts at human security it is to be expected both that their idealism will parallel the idealism of the world and that their actual programmes and panaceas, like their social diagnoses, will be deeply materialistic. However, in reality, the more society is offered material improvement as an anodyne for the ills of existence, the more it is rendered incapable of coping with the unavoidable suffering that is inseparable from life.

Modern society demonstrates a kind of spiritual disorientation. People rail against the sufferings they experience and call for collective or political solutions. These are not available, and the result is the accumulation of a permanent – but not, alas, a creative – discontent. The Church ought to step in with its timeless truths about the spiritual nature of man and the worthlessness of human attempts at security. Life was meant to be hazardous, and it will always be unjust, because the calculation of social justice is set upon grounds that relate not to some definable absolute but to the shifting sands of human expectations.

The impact of nuclear weapons should have had a similar effect. They should have reminded men of their moral frailty and of the impermanence of their passage through the world. Instead there is a headlong rush, now joined by much religious opinion, to place survival above ideology, and to see the world made 'safe' again, at whatever cost to the values human society exists to cultivate.

The Church exists to witness the priority of the personal over the political. It knows what the modern world seems so anxious to ignore: that most of the ills that afflict mankind are not susceptible to political solutions. It knows that personal disappointments, grave illness, family dislocations, frustrated ambition, and so forth – the very materials of daily existence, in fact – are not cured by manipulating the environment. It beholds the failed utopias which litter the human record but which still have renewed appeal.'

The Synod met in November 1984 to debate a report from the Church of England's Board of Social Responsibility entitled 'Perspectives on Economics'. It was the opportunity not only for the Bishop of Durham to make his maiden speech to the Church's parliament from the bench of bishops but also for the whole Church establishment to air its doubts about the course of economic medicine being dispensed by the Conservative government. If it was once true that the Anglican Church was the Tory Party at prayer it was no longer. The joke going the rounds was that it was now the S.D.P. at prayer and the general tone of the debate on the economy was such that there was much truth in the jest.

A consensus emerged from the gathering of the Synod as they met at Westminster. It was that the government under Mrs Thatcher lacked humanity. The Bishop of Durham's eagerly anticipated contribution was much in line with the mood of the day.

First the Bishop of Lincoln, the Right Reverend Simon Phipps, opened the debate in his capacity as Chairman of the Industrial and Economic Affairs Committee. He called for a political initiative to tackle unemployment.

To quote *The Times* report, Simon Phipps said that, while the Government had had remarkable success in bringing down inflation, the side effect, which had not at first surfaced as a political issue, was severe unemployment, including long-term unemployment.

'I believe that it is not enough just to say, as the Government does, that the revival of the economy, on the basis of the greater efficiency they have engendered, will produce the jobs required to reduce unemployment,' he said.

The philosophy of a free market could be a useful economic tool, but it could not be made to symbolize a whole philosophy of life without doing damage, he said. Industrial relations had to take into consideration the nature of men and women and not just the levels of wages and prices.

'Most important of all', he said, 'is when a nation is unavoidably faced with making painful changes, that the Government should seek to build up as great a climate of confidence and mutual understanding as may be possible within which those changes will be the more easily able to be faced. . . .

'When a society, a nation, an institution, an industry, pulls together and not apart,' he said, 'something new emerges within it which is for the common best.'

The public gallery was full and the television lights ablaze when David Jenkins rose. He read from a prepared text and the style was unmistakable. It was delivered in an urgent and earnest tone and contained the usual number of quotable, pithy and colourful phrases. The government's economic policies had become 'a false faith, an idolatry,' was one. Another much quoted was this, 'If acting on monetarist principles steadily increases the number of the poor and makes the rich even richer then it must be challenged.' It qualified as an *Observer* 'quote of the week'. But one remark above all stuck and was to follow the Bishop around for weeks after and would threaten to undermine the credibility of everything he had said. Talking of a certain Sunderland family he claimed that 'the children have to take it in turns to go to school at the moment as they only have one pair of shoes between them'. It is well worth quoting the speech in full:

'Mr Chairman, I am clear that we should welcome this report heartily and use it urgently. It helps us as we face up to the way in which economic affairs and economic policies shape our society and the lives of ourselves and our neighbours. Appeals for humane values, or concern for communities are liable to be dismissed as woolly on the grounds that such appeals ignore "economic realities". We must therefore become a little more instructed about the alleged realities of economics. We are in danger of being told that the way we can love our neighbours is determined by "economic realities".

'Of course, there is some real truth in this. If 30 per cent or more of our neighbours are unemployed, then an essential component of love for our neighbours will be facing up to the real possibilities of production, availability of resources and so on. Corporate care needs resources to match individual love and respect in meeting people's needs and in convincing them that they continue to belong and have a share in whatever our society produces and possesses. Thus, in the recent correspondence between Mr Peter Walker and myself, Mr Walker was entirely right to challenge me to debate about the connection between compassion and efficiency.

'Such a debate must be conducted as an urgent critique of present practice and an urgent search for better practice. Here, I would like to draw the attention of Synod to the most theologically important part of the document before us. This is contained in the section "Assessing the Schools" (i.e. of economic thought and prescription). The theologically significant crux is summed up in 4.18 – "unfortunately . . . clear answers to these questions are not generally forthcoming. One possibility is that there exists no definite answer, however good the analytic tools."

'This illustrates from the economic sphere, a general point about the human condition which Christian faith requires us to stress and enables us to face. We are limited creatures with limited knowledge (as well as limited good will). So we can never be *sure* about any of our theorizing, modelling and prescribing. This goes with our being in the Image of God. So we can always live in hope and under

131

the challenge of the love, justice and freedom of God. Thus we have to face and insist that others – especially those with power – should face the provisionality of our theories, including those about economic realities and the prescriptions we draw from them. Theories contain an element of faith and an element of choice about the values we intend to promote. They are never guaranteed prescriptions drawn from inevitable descriptions of reality. If acting on monetarist principles steadily increases the number of the poor and makes the rich even richer then it must be challenged. It is no answer to say "but this is the only way forward". This is as dogmatic as the claims of Marxist socialism about the necessity of the Party to promote the good of the People, so that bureaucratic inefficiency and totalitarian violence are both necessary and justified. The costs of any policy are part of the grounds for judging it, and possibly, of opposing it. A faith about economics or about politics which insists that all sorts of social costs and personal sufferings are justified now because we are surely right, the world is like this and this is the only realistic programme, is a false faith, in fact an idolatry. So, as Christians and worshippers of God we have to be ready to engage in these economic and political debates.

'I would just like to add that there is great individual urgency about this as well as corporate and collective urgency. Present policies may be held to be the most economically hopeful we can get but people are suffering acutely. I asked one of the advice bureaus which are working hard among the poor and unemployed in my diocese to let me have some typical cases which show the effects of recession combined with the cuts in social security upon individuals. This is the third case presented to me. It concerns a Sunderland family, living on one of the outlying estates.

' "The family comprises a husband and wife and two sons aged 10 and 12. The husband was made redundant 14 months ago after 19 years work in the shipyards. The wife does not work and the only income the family has is a total of £9.48 per day which has to feed the family, clothe the family, pay for all other household expenses such as fuel for heating and lighting and the replacement of things like lightbulbs, etc. This is proving harder and harder as time goes by and with winter approaching the wife does not know how they will be able to pay their next electricity bill.

' "The children have to take it in turns to go to school at the moment as they only have one pair of shoes between them. The family is hoping to be able to afford another pair in the next few weeks, but it remains to be seen whether or not this will be possible.

' "In late October the husband, who has been receiving treatment for severe depression, took an overdose. He spent a few days in hospital but is now out again. He says that although it might appear to be a coward's way out, it seemed a better idea than going on living. At least, he said, his wife would be entitled to the long-term rate of Supplementary Benefit which is worth an extra £7 per week. The family will not qualify for this as long as he is living with them. That extra £7 could have bought his younger son the pair of shoes that he needs to go to school."

'Now, hard cases make bad laws but there are thousands and probably tens of thousands of such cases. The Prophet Amos said: 'Thus saith the Lord . . . I will not turn away the punishment thereof because they sold the righteous for silver and the poor for a pair of shoes" (Amos 2:6).

'Debates on economic perspectives are very necessary and they are very urgent. Theories about economics have become the expression of a faith and of a way of dealing with men and women and the world. We, as Christians, cannot afford to leave that faith and commitment uncriticized or unchallenged. The matter is of the utmost political and public urgency. It is also of the utmost personal and individual urgency for literally millions of people. I hope that Synod will enthusiastically commend this Report.'

It was a speech to delight Fleet Street. The *Daily Mirror* reported it under the headline 'BISHOP SLAMS THATCHER'S POOR LAW' and reported the family case-history unquestioningly. The Tory press however seized the opportunity to undercut the whole of the critique by challenging the story of the two Sunderland children with one pair of shoes between them. The *Daily Mail* claimed that welfare officials in Sunderland 'could scarcely believe it when they heard the bishop's remarks on radio'. They quoted a council spokesman as saying 'our reaction is one of incredulity. There are so many provisions which could be made for a family like this. There are national and local funds including the Lord Major's fund for needy children. If the Bishop had come to us we could have helped.' An inquiry, the *Daily Mail* reported, had been launched by the chairman of the local social services committee. The paper also reported that one of the welfare workers who had briefed the Bishop at the Advice and Support Centre in Sunderland confirmed that while, for reasons of confidentiality he could not identify the family by name, they were by no means exceptional.

For a while there was an unsavoury Fleet Street scramble to find the family, but the Bishop stood by the story when challenged and with hindsight had no regrets at quoting it.

The rest of the Synod debate for all its value was something of an anti-climax after David Jenkins. It did, however, contain some important and useful contributions from the Archbishop of York, the Dean of St Paul's and Canon Peter Boulton of Worksop who was applauded for his claim that the industrial relations policy of the National Coal Board was completely shattered, with the advent of Mr Ian MacGregor, by the introduction of an alien, harsh, old-fashioned and authoritarian form of industrial relations which was well calculated to upset the N.U.M.

In the following days it was impossible for the government to ignore the shock-waves of the debate taking place just a few yards away from parliament, Whitehall and the political party headquarters. The chance to reply to the concerted criticism came a few days later when the Conservative Party Chairman, John Selwyn Gummer (who is also a member of Synod) had an invitation to preach at Great St Mary, Cambridge. His sermon too, printed and distributed in advance by the party press office, contained colourful and pithy quotes every bit as spicey as those of the Bishop of Durham. The authority of bishops, he said, was episcopal and not technical. 'They can no more pontificate on economics than the Pope could correct Galileo on physics.'

Mr Gummer was dismissive of the case of the Sunderland family. Far from there being thousands and tens of thousands of cases, he said, the Bishop, when challenged, 'could not even find the case which he had described in such graphic detail. He'd heard it all second hand.'

Nobody in Sunderland [to quote the *Daily Telegraph* report of Mr Gummer's sermon] had identified the family and the welfare authorities said they would immediately ensure that any such children would be properly clothed.

'Now what pains me about this is not that it embarrasses the Tory Government. It is that it cheapens the Church.'

Mr Gummer said that in recent weeks 'many of us have been deeply embarrassed by the continuing examples of bishops who have believed that it is enough to get the sentiments right without bothering too much about the facts'.

Mr Gummer referred to the call by the Archbishop of Canterbury, Dr Robert Runcie, and the Roman Catholic Archbishop of Westminster, Cardinal Hume, for an emergency Government airlift to Ethiopia.

He added: 'The day after their pronouncement, the Save the Children Fund had to point out that the Church had not done its homework – had not checked what a Hercules transport plane could carry and what the Ethiopian logistical problems involved.'

Mr Gummer told the Cambridge congregation that bishops 'must challenge our economic aims and our political purposes and must challenge our priorities and question our political aims.'

But they could not 'call upon politicians to choose Keynesian economics over monetarism or any other system'. Their authority was episcopal not technical.

Mr Gummer added: 'They must, however, insist that we make our choice with the claims of the Gospel clearly in mind.

'The Bishop of Durham is plain Mr Jenkins when he gives me his political views. 'The problem is that he confuses Mr Jenkins with the Bishop of Durham and that confusion lies at the heart of many of the Church's current pronouncements.

'When a Bishop describes the chairman of the National Coal Board, Mr Ian MacGregor, as an imported, elderly American and seeks for his replacement by some local product, he uses the language which can only wound and shock rather than challenge any change. They are not the words of a reconciler. They are the rhetoric of political debate . . . When Churchmen have controversial things to say, they must not say them in a way which wounds. They must not . . . demean themselves by personal attacks.

Within twenty-four hours David Jenkins replied and was embroiled in his second public debate with a leading member of the Conservative party. He was speaking at Middlesbrough Town Hall. Government condemnation of church leaders, who questioned its policies, he said, would lead to the death of true politics. To quote *The Guardian* report of 20 November:

Raising a criticism of a particular policy or government

was not the same thing as belonging to the opposite party, 'or especially to be adhering to some extreme, possibly imaginary, view of what politics and life are about,' Bishop Jenkins said.

'If every time a genuine question is raised, based on a combination of a reading of the facts and of a faith in God, about the effects of some policy, and then one is accused, if the government is to the right, of being nearly Communist, and if the party is to the left of being some rabid Conservative, this is the death of true politics, and of all hope for community.

'The Church in particular has the right and a duty to put questions to people in power and to people with opportunities of influencing politics,' he said.

The bishop criticised 'Bolshevik sects' and Government policies which, he said, were destroying the common good in local government.

'There are notorious examples of tightly-organised, sectarian left-wing factions obtaining control of councils and using this control to ensure that only what might be called fully paid-up and authentically card-carrying members of the correct Bolshevik sect have access to office, information, or resources,' he said.

'I sometimes think that we ordinary, local human beings are in danger of being left with scarcely any choice between left-wing sects which threaten us with a Kremlin and right-wing governments which threaten us with Whitehall.'

By coincidence, the same night as David Jenkins was speaking in Middlesbrough, another new bishop was preaching as a guest at a packed and overflowing St Paul's Cathedral in London. The new Bishop of Johannesburg, the Right Reverend Desmond Tutu, also condemned the separation of religion and politics. A God who required such a division, he said, would be 'an aloof figure dwelling in an Olympian fastness unconcerned about his people'.

137

In general, apart from attracting the echoes of a number of members of his own party, Mr Gummer's sermon produced surprisingly little support. Indeed it was revealed that some 5,500 grants had been made that year from the Mayor's Charity Fund in Sunderland, and one of the local clergy defended the 'tone and accuracy' of the Bishop's story.

The *Daily Star* attempted to breathe new life into the controversy on 30 November by running a headline, 'Where are those barefoot boys, Bishop?' The paper reported an angry Sunderland Council leader, Charles Slater, attacking the Bishop's comments as 'casting a slur' on the council's efforts to care for its people.

> All efforts by our education and social services departments to trace these boys have been to no avail.
>
> If the family exists the bishop should reveal their identity immediately.
>
> If he or others tell us who the boys are we will take action to relieve them of their distress within twenty-four hours.
>
> 'I give my personal guarantee that the family's case will be dealt with in strict confidentiality.'
>
> Council officials ordered forty field officers to try to trace the family and school registers have been checked, but no clue has been found.
>
> However the bishop, Dr David Jenkins, still claims the brothers exist.
>
> And staff at the Ford and Pennywell Advice Centre, Sunderland, are adamant that the barefoot brothers exist.
>
> Centre staff worker Billy Jackson said the family's identity was being kept secret because of fears for the father's mental health.
>
> He added: 'It was us who told the bishop about the brothers.'
>
> Social services director Bob Hankinson said: 'It may

well be that we could offer this family some help, but
their identity is being withheld from us.'

All requests to the Bishop for details of the case were
referred by him to the Ford and Pennywell Advice Centre
who flatly refused to break the family's confidence. The
centre did however allow a local paper reporter to interview
another typical family on an anonymous basis. The interview confirmed that dire poverty still existed in the middle
of welfare-state Britain but did not satisfy the Bishop's
critics who still wanted chapter and verse on the specific
case he had raised in Synod.

The miners' strike of course continued well into 1985.
Although the Bishop kept a close eye on the progress of the
dispute in his diocese and nationwide, he did not remain
at centre-stage in the affair. However, in January he did
call for a compromise and said that it was likely the government was preventing the Coal Board from negotiating, and
right at the end of February he was prepared to go on
record saying that the cost of the strike was now out of all
proportion to anything they might have gained and that
they were, almost literally, destroying themselves. He told
students at his old university at Leeds (to quote the *Yorkshire
Post*):

Unless argument is kept going, you are heading for the
death of politics – and that is dictatorship.
    In a seeming oblique reference to Thatcherite policies,
he said: 'We need to remind ourselves very strongly that
we go back to dogmatism at very great cost.
    'Whether it be dogmatism of religion or dogmatism of
politics. I firmly believe there will be hell to pay.'
    Bishop Jenkins said one reason why the country was
'in a mess' over politics was that people expected too
much of politics.
    'Politics is always a matter of compromise on prin-
ciples,' he said.

139

But there seemed to be a tremendous despair of politics in Britain today – a despair shown by the great number of pressure groups in the country.

The Bishop told the students: 'You must argue and protest against the tendency not to argue. You must also maintain an attack on the current party system to bring things in the direction of proportional representation.

A few days earlier the Bishop had become involved in public debate with yet another leading Conservative. He had taken the occasion of the Second Reading of the Transport Bill in the House of Lords to repeat to the Transport Secretary warnings he had made shortly before, when speaking in the north-east, giving the grounds for grave disquiet over the moral, political and practical implications of the proposal to open up local bus services to private competition. In referring to the government's view of competition, he again made a reference to idolatry, of promoting that which is good to a role that has the status of God. If compassion is excluded, he said, 'you've got a destructive God'. The moral disquiet lay with the valid question which could be put to the proponents of the bill as to whether they were putting their faith in a simplified view of the market and asking that faith to bear more than it should or could on a very doubtful principle.

The Transport Secretary, Mr Nicholas Ridley, had already made his response clear when the Bishop had said it all earlier in his Middlesbrough speech. Mr Ridley said the Bishop had misunderstood the Bill, which would still allow local authorities to provide concessionary fares and did not affect total levels of subsidy.

'I am concerned', he said to the Bishop, 'that you seem to feel it right to add fuel to the feeling of alienation between the north and the south. If reconciliation is to be achieved, then steps in the right direction have to be acknowledged and welcomed.'

On 26 February, David Jenkins wrote to Mr Ridley from

Bishop Auckland. He thanked him for taking his arguments seriously and continued:

> . . . details of the effects of total deregulation apart, I still cannot see how equating the supply of local transport services to the supply of groceries is anything but a false and unrealistic analogy. Nor can I see how a 'free market' could create the means of supplying the North East, in its present poverty-stricken state, with the minimal transport services it urgently needs to sustain any sort of standard of life . . . . Most practically and urgently it seems to me that your proposals are most likely to destroy what transport network there is and that, at the very least, it is essential to introduce competition stage by stage via tendering and to leave powers of regulation.

The patience of the Prime Minister finally snapped in March. She had listened to bishops in general, and David Jenkins in particular, criticizing almost every aspect of her political philosophy. They had not confined themselves to broad brush-strokes of general disquiet but had picked over individual pieces of specialist legislation. Not even her rural transport policy was spared. In March however, David Jenkins had gone further than any other bishop had dared, in saying that Britain under its first woman Prime Minister, Mrs Thatcher, was heading for a police state.

He talked to a meeting in Newcastle-upon-Tyne of 'our present sense of outrage about a divided society'. But the straw which broke the back of Mrs Thatcher's patience was another appearance on LWT's 'Credo' on Channel 4. He was interviewed by John Stapleton at the end of a programme reviewing the current state of Church–Government relations. The transcript of the interview on the page shows up again all the Bishop's faults as a communicator, his muddled construction and garbled out-spilling of ideas. In the years since his first 'Credo' appearance he had not improved his presentation. Yet the sense and urgency of what he was saying was conveyed, and again there were quotable nuggets for the popular press. For example, he claimed government ministers seem 'to be continually showing not only that they don't care but that they don't seem to care that they don't seem to care'. To quote from the interview:

JOHN STAPLETON: Bishop, churchleaders like yourself seem to be calling for a compromise between the demands of efficiency and the obligations that flow from compassion. Could we just examine the parameters of that compromise – what, for example, would you like the Government to do differently?

DAVID JENKINS: Well for one thing the Government should be much clearer about what it is asking of people and how it is exacting things of the people who are already not well-off. It would therefore for instance follow, I think, that the Government should be much more sensitive about requiring a compromise for the people who are better off, perhaps not compromised, actual costs from the people who are better off, such as for instance the whole business of higher rates of tax and the higher business of mortgage reliefs and so on, so that it looks as if, in fact it is, the costs are being more widely borne over the community. The second thing would be that the Government should compromise in its confrontational attitude to trade unions; . . . if you insist on treating the organization of the working of the workers as enemies, the cost of that in social disruption has to be taken account.

JOHN STAPLETON: What sort of compromise are you talking about with regard to the unions, Bishop?

DAVID JENKINS: The sort of compromise I'm thinking of from the unions is to take very seriously this business that they can price themselves out of a job . . . but you can't expect unions, it seems to me, to face up to those sort of realities unless it's clear that the Government understands and is prepared to make concessions on its own front.

JOHN STAPLETON: Could we just move to what you might think the Government should do for the worse off. And presumably a change of policy in that direction obviously means a different priority with regard to spending power. What sort of things would you like the Government to do to help those people?

DAVID JENKINS: It seems to me there are three things. The first is, of course, there is a major concern for wealth creation; the second thing is that there is a major concern for wealth distribution, that is to say the social shares, but the third thing is, and this is what I think is often forgotten, there is the effect on wealth creation and so on of social cost, and if you get an increasing number of people who seem to be excluded from society and every time you make a cut for the sake of wealth creation, that cut makes them more miserable, then you've got a series of costs here which need to be taken account of prudentially. I mean, how does the Government expect to maintain a viable society if three million, four million, five million people are forced into further and further misery? Maintaining the social services, for instance, for the badly off is a necessary investment in the future. It may push the recovery future further off – or seem to – but unless you're prepared to put this sort of investment in, I don't see that you'll get a recovery future . . .

JOHN STAPLETON: Let's pursue our conversation about help for the unemployed. Would you, for example, advocate giving unemployed more in benefit?

DAVID JENKINS: I am much inclined to think that it isn't a question of raising the benefits above a certain level, but

143

it is much more a question of building up both a social atmosphere, and a social structure in which people who are unemployed – and of course receiving a sufficient minimum benefit – are given some sense that they still very much belong to society, and that there are efforts in society, both to sympathize with their plight, and to actually help them . . .

I think there's a total failure, or at worst, nearly total failure, in the corridors of power, down in the south, to appreciate really how bitter people are feeling. And this just as, in inner cities, you get riots and so on, you could throw the social divisiveness into a much more violent form, quite easily.

JOHN STAPLETON: What you're suggesting, of course, many people would sympathize with. Many people would say, Well, all well and good, but all of these things and most of these things anyway are going to cost a great deal of money. Where do you suggest that money comes from?

DAVID JENKINS: Again, I can't go into detail in that, but I mean a series of things occur to me. You see, the options that are taken in using the money we have, are political decisions, and are not absolutely essential. I mean, there are what you might call the elementary things, which benefit the middle classes and above, and don't benefit the lower classes. Those are things like rates of tax, and mortgage relief and so on. And then there are much sharper and much more difficult questions. I mean, if you choose to have Trident, you choose to pay for what is called an independent deterrent, and therefore for national pride, at a very great cost. Now, is that the right sort of choice to take about national pride, or should you choose much more for building up the community?

JOHN STAPLETON: As you raise the question of choices, let me ask you to make a choice. If the choice was between actually putting the defence of the nation at risk, and helping or giving more help to the unemployed, what would your choice be, and what choice do you think the Government should make? '

DAVID JENKINS: Well, I think the defence of the nation is at risk anyway, that we are not capable of doing more than making a contribution to our own defence. It seems to me that the whole business of an independent nuclear deterrent is a piece of – wasteful piece of over national pride. So I would have no hesitation in suggesting that the Government should risk the defence thing for the community thing.

JOHN STAPLETON: I'm sure many people will share your concern, but would still be rather puzzled, as to what your alternative strategy would be.

DAVID JENKINS: I haven't got an alternative strategy. It isn't my job to have an alternative strategy. It is my job to press people with the moral issues, with the prudential issues, with the political choices – to draw attention to some political choices, such as for instance spending all this money in keeping 1,500 people in the Falkland Islands, when we can't spend money to deal with four million unemployed, and so on, These are sharp moral choices which people should be aware we are making. And I do not believe that the parameters are anything like as determined as the Government claims.

JOHN STAPLETON: Are you suggesting that the Government should abandon its Fortress Falklands policy, as it is called?

DAVID JENKINS: I am drawing attention to the fact that there's a moral choice here quite as much as elsewhere, and that to choose to invest X million pounds a day in Fortress Falklands is a moral choice, because you say for the sake of those 1,500 people and certain principles of international justice you're going to spend that money, but you won't spend money for the sake of X million unemployed people and other forms of justice, and therefore people must be aware they choose. . . .

I don't think the government is insincere. I think that in all probability they're wrong, and in particular that they have for reasons – part of it to do no doubt with their class and their circumstances and their tendency, as we all do, to favour our friends and so on they do seem to be continually showing, not only that they don't care, but they don't seem to care, and they don't seem to care that they don't seem to care – because of these various manoeuvres which fit into one policy but keep on cutting against the people who are already hard off.

JOHN STAPLETON: So the sort of society we should be creating is what?

DAVID JENKINS: The sort of society we should be creating is one that we don't yet know about. I'm sure we've got to go into a great period of turbulence and uncertainty, and so I can't, wouldn't want to fault the government on the grounds that may be it won't come off, because may be other things won't come off. It's the sort of society which remains convinced that, while politics is about power, it isn't only about power. It is also about community and altruism, and there are resources that can be drawn out of people if they're given the chance to work at their own level and their own problems, even under conditions of great hardship and no work and so on – signs of which can be seen in things like little co-operatives that are growing up, all sorts of small-business innovations, things the government's encouraged, self-help groups and all the rest of it, which could move us towards what you might call a labour-intensive caring society, which had to live averagely at a lower standard than now, but because people cared for one

146

another they found point in it and might then be in a position to take off again in whatever is the next stage.

JOHN STAPLETON: Is what you're suggesting this, that in your view as a Christian it is far better to have perhaps a society that produces less, that in which there is a much more equitable share of the wealth, than a society that actually produces a great deal, but under which a few people suffer?

DAVID JENKINS: You mean a few people benefit and many people suffer. I think I am saying that a combination of my insight as a Christian on the moral side of things, with my judgement as an ordinary prudential citizen, is that a society, in which you get fewer and fewer people with more and more wealth and more and more people who are at the bottom of the heap, and no chance of joining in, is not a viable society. And that is one of prudential and practical ways in which moral issues are raised. That we are in fact much more members of one another, including the productive purposes and wealth creation purposes, and that this is a factor which has to be brought in.

JOHN STAPLETON: Is what you're saying, Bishop, that you have a rather different view of human nature than Mrs Thatcher?

DAVID JENKINS: Well, I'm not at all sure, because I think most Conservatives agree with Christians about having a fairly poor view of human nature in the sense of having to take original sin carefully, so that you know you better have the market to check people and so on. I think she's in one way good on sin, so people have to be checked, but then she's over-optimistic about what a few people can do. I think I have a more communal view of society, which should insist that you've got to invest more in society as a whole, and not concentrate simply on the individual.

147

Mrs Thatcher waited until the Saturday to give her scornful response. She was in a fiery mood addressing the party faithful of the Conservative Central Council. She had both bishops and dons in her sights as she fired – the dons because Oxford University had just recently declined to award her the customary honorary degree as a prime minister. David Jenkins was both bishop and don. Mrs Thatcher delighted her followers, and the *Sunday Express* ran an article headed, 'MAGGIE BLASTS "CUCKOO BISHOPS" ':

'There is a consistent tendency', she said, 'in our society to downgrade the creators of wealth, and nowhere is this attitude more marked than in cloister and common room.

'What these critics apparently can't stomach is that wealth creators have a tendency to acquire wealth in the process of creating it for others.'

To laughter and applause the Prime Minister went on: 'You may have noticed that recently the voices of some reverend and right reverend prelates have been heard in the land.

'I make no complaint about that. After all, it wouldn't be spring, would it, without the voice of the occasional cuckoo!

'You may have noticed, too, that these clerical voices have been ranging fairly confidently into the sphere of economic management with their quite detailed advice.'

Mrs Thatcher, who was speaking at Newcastle-upon-Tyne, after thus by inference slamming the Bishop of Durham, Dr David Jenkins – though she did not name him – said she would refer to the Parable of the Talents and pointed out: 'Those who traded with their talents, and multipled them, were those who won approval. And the essence of their performance was the willingness to take risks to make a gain.

'That spirit of risk-taking and enterprise is coming back today. No Government in years has made enterprise so worthwhile as this one.'

It could well be argued that Mrs Thatcher is closer to the feeling of ordinary church members in the pew than the bishops. Churchgoing in many areas is often biased towards the more affluent and the middle classes, Mrs Thatcher's own people. Anglican churches in working-class areas are often poorly attended. High Church attendance figures are found in areas which also tend to return a Conservative member of parliament. In the same way the theological debate in academic circles had over the years become increasingly alien to the people in the pews on Sunday, so the bishops in their debating of social issues have left many of the faithful behind. For instance, Gallup Poll published in *The Daily Telegraph* in April 1985 asked Anglicans this question: 'Do you think the Church should keep out of political matters or should it express its views on day-to-day social and political questions?' 58 per cent of Anglicans thought church leaders should not express their views. Interestingly, replies varied according to age. While 51 per cent of Anglicans under twenty-five believed the Church should not get involved the figure rose to 64 per cent of those aged sixty-five or above.

When asked whether any of the recent controversial comments by prominent people in the Church of England had made them feel more or less favourable towards the Church, 13 per cent said more favourable, 25 per cent less favourable, and the remainder, 62 per cent, had either been unaffected or had not heard enough to judge.

One in three of those who had become less favourable to the Church cited comments by the Bishop of Durham, specifically on the miners' strike.

14

The sermons

The ability to turn the memorable phrase is an invaluable one in these days of instant television and radio news. It is David Jenkins' particular gift to be able to find the quotable quote, but as he discovered on at least one occasion there are risks attached. Sometimes a phrase can be taken quite out of context, given a life of its own, and takes on a quite different meaning from that originally intended.

In October 1984, David Jenkins was invited to appear on a BBC Radio 4 programme, 'Poles Apart'. It was a programme built around the idea of putting a controversial figure in a hot-seat and letting him or her face questions, sometimes hostile ones, from opponents. It was recorded in the library of Auckland Castle, and inevitably he was asked to state and defend his views on the resurrection and virgin birth, in the course of which he was to produce the phrase reported in the newspapers as 'conjuring tricks with bones' to describe the reported physical events of the resurrection.

David Jenkins was asked why, if things were believable symbolically and God worked in history, a symbol in history might not be seen as 'real'. He replied,

'It is real, that's the point. All I said was literally physical. I was very careful in the use of language. After all a conjuring trick with bones only proves that somebody's clever at a conjuring trick with bones. I am bothered about what I call God and conjuring tricks. I am not clear that

150

God manoeuvres physical things. I am clear that he works miracles through personal responses and faith. . . .

'You can't have a religious view about reality and another view about daily life. Therefore my faith in God forces me to raise these questions about the virgin birth and the resurrection. I am not saying people do not get unto God through these various things. I am saying it should not be laid down that you must get onto God that way.'

He said that the Gospels were not 'literal news – like accounts of a set of events.

'I am quite clear God has not abandoned reality and history after the first century or even after the fourth century, and therefore to insist that in order to be a Christian you have to think in the way in which the New Testament people thought, still less that you have to think in the way the fourth-century people thought is simply a lack of faith in God. It is to deny God in history and it is to fail in our mission.'

In fairness to David Jenkins, his comment after the programme – as a super-charged row broke out with charges of blasphemy being levelled against him – should be added. In *The Daily Telegraph* of 29 October he is reported as saying, 'I am beginning to believe that some of the media are populated by people who can only read two or three words at a time and therefore quote everything out of context. What I actually said was that the resurrection was far more than a conjuring trick with bones, which is the exact opposite of what I have been quoted as saying.' And he added that anyone who had heard the whole programme as transmitted would find the controversy 'ridiculous'. He would still carry on saying excitable things, he said, 'that is exactly what Jesus used to do and so I could not have a better example to follow.'

But the phrase 'conjuring trick with bones', however

meant, was the one which stuck in people's minds from the moment it was released as part of a package of press preview quotes. An angry letter was sent by Mrs Mary Whitehouse of the 'Viewers and Listeners Association' to the Archbishop of Canterbury asking him to disassociate himself from the Bishop of Durham and offer him the chance to return to university life. The Conservative M.P., Mr Nicholas Winterton, denounced 'the diabolically blasphemous phrase' and described the bishop as 'a dangerous joker who by some error has been allowed to creep into the congregation of bishops'.

The Lord Chancellor, Lord Hailsham contributed an opinion, 'These comments serve only to undermine the simple, honest faith of those who are far better Christians than David Jenkins. I much prefer the word of Matthew, Mark, Luke and John because they were there and David Jenkins wasn't.'

Two other Conservative M.P.s were roused. Sir William Clark said, 'His ignorance about the Bible nearly matches his ignorance about how to handle the miner's strike. . . . I shall seek to raise in Parliament the whole question of how bishops come to be appointed.' And Nicholas Fairbairn described the Bishop's utterances as 'deadly offensive . . . he is saying Christianity is a giant confidence trick'.

From the bench of bishops and the evangelical quarter came words which perhaps carried greater weight. Michael Baughen, Bishop of Chester, was quoted in the *Sunday Express* as saying that David Jenkins' remarks were 'an appalling insult to my Lord . . . not only erroneous but immensely damaging'.

In the same Sunday newspaper a week later, David Jenkins was quoted as saying that anyone who said he, David Jenkins, did not believe in the resurrection and incarnation of Jesus was 'a liar'. He had delivered a 'fierce and categorical' statement of his adherence to orthodox belief to his diocesan synod in Durham.

'I do believe in the resurrection of Jesus Christ our Lord from the dead.

'I myself live in hope of resurrection. I do believe that Jesus Christ is both God for us and man with us.

'Anyone who says that I do not believe in the resurrection and in the incarnation is a liar. This I must say fiercely and categorically.'

Questions about the literal truth of the story of the virgin birth and precise physical happenings associated with the resurrection were separate from and secondary to 'the fundamental Christian beliefs that God raised up Jesus and that Jesus Christ is to be received and worshipped as God became man and the man who is God,' he said.

The Bishop denied he was attacking 'simple faith' and 'simple believers'.

He was simply asking 'simple believers' to recognize there was more than one way of believing.

And as *The Daily Telegraph* reported the Synod, all Bishop Jenkins was asking of simple believers was that they have faith enough to recognize three things:

'One – there is more than one way of believing, of exploring belief, and of expressing belief.

'Two – everyone has the right to explore belief in a different way from "simple believers". (Mystery, after all, is great.)

'Three – some people have to believe in a different way. God's dealings with all his people cannot possibly be defined or limited by the way he has, so far, dealt with me.'

He added 'There is no final and absolutely defining authority available to Christians, only a set of authorities (notably as that great Anglican Hooker would remind us, Scripture, Tradition and a sound use of reason), which Christians again and again have to consult.'

However, one gets an incomplete picture of David Jenkins' faith from the quotable quotes. Much of the background to his current position is argued out in his works published some fifteen, twenty and more years ago. *Living with Questions* was first published in 1969 and is a collection of sermons and papers dating from 1956. Part of it is a response to the 'Honest to God' debate. *The Glory of Man* was published in 1967 and consists of his Bampton Lectures reprinted. In 1966 his *Guide to the Debate about God* was published, and in 1970 the work *What is Man?*

His current position can best be understood from the series of considered papers and sermons delivered as bishop. They start, with the enthronement sermon and include addresses to Synod, contributions to the diocesan publication, *The Durham Lamp*, various sermons and the Hibbert Lecture. They represent his current position better than any of his off-the-cuff statements, and up-date his previously published works.

His letter in *The Durham Lamp* of December 1984 was entitled 'Christmas and the Challenge of Faith'. He wrote of the wonder and majesty of the Christmas story and then said that he hoped he would not be spoiling Christmas for his readers by raising questions, but he had to challenge them and himself to faith. Unlike the story of Father Christmas, the story of the birth of Jesus, he said, had to be told 'for real'. The Bible stories were 'for real', not by being literally true but by being the inspired symbols of a living faith about the real activity of God. No statement about God, David Jenkins said, can be simply literally true as God cannot be pinned down or defined in ordinary language. To insist on witnessing to God in simple language was something very close to magic and superstition.

Then, in one of his quotable quotes he said, 'We have no right to insist on the literal truth of the story about the virgin birth of Jesus'. There was reason to believe, he said, that this was one of the embroideries. But, he added, we have every right to give thanks for the obedience of Mary,

154

chosen wonderfully and mysteriously by God to be personally one with us. He then quoted William Temple's *Readings
in St John's Gospel* on the subject of angels.

'It is not to be presumed that angels are physical objects
reflecting rays of light upon the retina of the eye. When
men "see or hear" angels, it is rather to be supposed
that an intense interior awareness of a divine message
leads to the projection of an image which is then experienced as an occasion of something seen and heard. That
divine messengers were sent and divine messages
received we need not doubt; that they took physical form
so that all who "saw" anything must "see" the same
thing we need not suppose.'

The Bishop of Durham concluded that while we had no
right to insist on the Bible accounts of shepherds, wise men
and so on being verbatim historical accounts, celebration
at Christmas should be convinced, unquestioning and open
to all the glory that the symbols, stories and confessions
point to now.

To wish one another happy Christmas, he said (this
time in his 1984 Christmas sermon), was to speak with
conviction and hope of the mystery of creation and birth,
of the mystery of ourselves and of the mystery of love who
is at once both God beyond all and the baby with all. The
real wonder of Christmas he said was not found in all the
extras, the star and the angels, but in the baby who grew
up to be Jesus of Nazareth who was to be crucified and
buried and raised up by God. At the first Christmas, he
explained, God put his seal of flesh and blood on the idea
of men and women being created in the image of God. God
came to share our human life.

The glory of God is to be glimpsed in every baby, David
Jenkins told his congregation, but this fact brought with it
a confrontation. Many babies are born into hunger or lack

of love. A living faith is bound to be disturbed and disturbing.

'We celebrate a baby as the glory of God. We know therefore that the physical energies, the chemical transactions and the genetic codes which have emerged within the universe are able not only to build up into the fragile and threatened glory of a human person but also into the receptacle, the vehicle, the embodiment, of the transcendent and eternal glory of God. Every unit of energy in the whole universe is permeated by the possibility of a personal purpose which comes alive in love and is to be fulfilled by love. No wonder therefore that an inspired writer, meditating on the meaning of the birth of the child who became both Lord and Christ, could write: "And suddenly there was with the angel a multitude of the heavenly host praising God and saying, Glory to God in the highest, and on earth peace among men with whom he is pleased!" (Luke 2:14).

'All is to be filled by the Glory of God, for all proceeds from the Glory of God who is love; and we, specks in the universe but persons in the image of God, have been called to know this glory, receive this glory and serve this glory. This is the message and the reality and the promise of the Baby who is the glory of God.'

Come Easter 1985, David Jenkins had written another article for *The Durham Lamp* and prepared a major Easter Day sermon. The challenge he set himself in his diocesan letter was to explain the meaning of the great Christian festival. He began by writing of Jesus's commitment to the sick and sinful, lost and rejected, to ordinary people in their frequent unhappiness, and how this caring, in the name of almighty God, disturbed the powers that be. Love, he suggested, was much more risky than either civil power or religious authority could cope with. So Jesus was crucified. Yet this time death and disillusion did not have the last word.

156

Those who had known and loved Jesus and put their hopes in him met him again. They met him in such a real and convincing way, and enough of them met him in enough different ways, for them to be absolutely sure that God had raised Jesus from the dead and that he was, not just resuscitated, but alive forever and part of the very life and eternity of God. As Paul puts it, 'We know that Christ, once raised from the dead, is never to die again: he is no longer under the dominion of death' (Romans 6:9, NEB). Here, in the resurrection of Jesus from the dead, is the evidence, the claim and the promise that human being and human living when given to love, when saved by love and when shaped by love, which is the love of God who is love, cannot be defeated or destroyed by sin, destruction and death, cannot be got down by governments, or religions, or sheer wretched ordinariness. Love is indeed open to life eternal, to fulfilment and enjoyment in the eternity and glory of God. 'O death, where is thy sting? O grave, where is thy victory?' (1 Corinthians 15:56, AV). They have been removed, for those who have faith, by the resurrection of Jesus Christ from the dead.

But to be able to write in such a positive way about the message of Easter did not necessarily mean that the bishop accepted the story of the empty tomb as an historical fact. He readily admitted he did not know if the tomb was empty or not. He also pointed out that an empty tomb did not prove the resurrection and as an event was not synonymous with the resurrection. In his Easter Day sermon, David Jenkins said that the Easter discovery was a growing and compelling discovery of the newness, 'the almightiness, the freedom and down-to-earthness of God'. He preached a vivid but very orthodox message of Easter. Yet it was his belief in the fact of the resurrection, while claiming that what physically happened to the body of the crucified Jesus was something no one could know with any historical

157

certainty, which confused many of the faithful. In an article he wrote at the time he asked the question 'what happened at the first Easter?', and began by saying with total conviction that the Easter message was simple and clear. Death could not put an end to Jesus.

He acknowleged that a gulf existed between two sorts of people, who believe with equal assurance and commitment in the resurrection.

The first group hold that stories told in the Gospels about encountering or seeing or discovering the risen Jesus are something very like careful newspaper reports of responsible eye-witness accounts of the details of incidents which, if you had been there, you would have seen and interpreted in the same way. It is further held that, by careful thought and reasonable speculation, these various stories can be built into a coherent and consistent account of the series of events and incidents which make-up the 'Resurrection of Jesus'.

The second group who, as I say, believe with equal assurance and commitment in the resurrection (I know because I belong to it!) do not see the Gospel stories in quite this way at all. They are convinced that detailed studies of the various stories make it clear that, first, they cannot be fitted into a consistent and coherent whole and that, secondly, like much else in the Bible, they show signs of being written up after the event to express faith and to convey a particular message or answer to a particular question. (A simple and obvious example is the way Mark's 'young man' gets turned into one angel and then two as story-tellers do their best to indicate how wonderful, important and God-guaranteed the resurrection of Jesus was and is. A point, of course, which all Christian believers share with the New Testament story-tellers, whether or not they hold them to be telling flatly literal stories or not.)

The second group of believers therefore hold that you

158

cannot tell precisely what happened at the first Easter nor get behind the experiences, encounters and discoveries of the early Church and their way of telling the stories of faith. What you can do is share their faith and enter into their (and subsequent generations of Christians') experiences of the risen Christ who gives us the knowledge of God's victory over sin and death through the Spirit. This faith includes the assurance, that whatever happened really, and was not just imagined, it makes all the difference in the world, and that the effects and the meaning of it will not be finally revealed or finally worked out until the End of the World.

And so it is that David Jenkins could conclude his Easter sermon with the words, 'the resurrection is neither to be pinned down nor to be wholly proved. It is to be lived by faith in the God who raised Jesus from the dead and who does and will raise up us with him. For "Christ is risen. He is risen indeed. Allelujah." '

15

'Fundamentalism fundamentally flawed'

The first year of David Jenkins' bishopric was one of great
event. Every public utterance was examined for its
newsworthy content, and the new bishop was reported as
having his say not only on doctrinal matters but political
and social issues as well, ranging from local buses to literacy
and numeracy. There was even a much quoted lapse of
language when he was reported as having criticized certain
community leaders for sitting on their 'arses and doing
nothing when things go wrong'. He was careful to disguise
some more colourful language shortly afterwards by
employing Latin. 'Nil illegitimi carborundum,' he urged an
audience; loosely translated, 'Don't let the bastards grind
you down.'

There was one occasion however when David Jenkins
found himself the centre of attention without having to
utter a word. The occasion was the February 1985 meeting
of the General Synod and a four-hour-long debate on the
nature of Christian belief. Despite the plea from the Bishop
of Winchester, John Taylor, that no one was on trial, there
was no shortage of accusers. A packed public gallery heard
the Reverend David Holloway say, 'We have a cancer in
the Church. In its early stages a cancer is hardly noticed
and is relatively easy to deal with. But, as it grows, it
gradually strangles the whole, and treatment is then trau-
matic. If it is not eradicated it brings death.'

The Church of England was at a crossroads, he alleged,
'the leadership had to make a choice. On the one hand,'

he said to the bench of bishops, 'you can continue on the path that was set by the Archbishop of York with the consecration of the Bishop of Durham in the full glare of public denials of the virgin birth and doubts over the empty tomb, without any prior disclaimers . . . or you can admit that Bishop Jenkins' consecration was wrong, that the virgin birth and the empty tomb are not optional as doctrines of the Church of England . . . If the Church of England has no doctrinal discipline, there will be growing disunity, numerical decline and sooner rather than later, financial deficits as church members vote increasingly not only with their feet but also with their cheque books.'

A barely disguised reference to David Jenkins was made by Philip Lovegrove, a Synod member from St Albans. He asked, 'When the Crown Appointments Commission appoints bishops, would they please not appoint bishops who stand up and say the Creed and give the impression that they have their fingers crossed behind their backs?'

David Jenkins listened, made notes and said nothing.

Sebastian Faulks of the *Sunday Telegraph* captured some of the atmosphere of the debate in a piece of witty, if absurd, sketch writing:

The Bishop of Durham lowered his head into his hands and kept it there. The General Synod, under the guise of a doctrinal debate, was out for his blood, and he knew it.

A hush fell on the company as the Archbishop of Canterbury took his place on the podium from where, we knew, he was preparing to deliver the fiercest theological rebuke since Sodom and Gomorrah.

The Synod members in the lifts at Church House on Wednesday wore clerical grey overcoats and sensible mufflers; they carried an odour of sanctity and Polo mints. But there was no mistaking the grimness of their purpose . . . .

161

And then suddenly, the scoreboard flickered in its moment of digital glory: 001. And in a flash of purple, retribution arrived at the microphone in the shape of Dr Runcie, the man whose marriage of the Prince and Princess of Wales caused one unkind critic to remark that he had single-handedly put the unction back into function.

He shot from the hip. A bishop, he said, must be a guardian of tradition and a guarantee of historic continuity. On the other hand, a bishop must also be an interpreter of tradition – a man of doubt, as far from the clear certainties of the celestial city as the rest of us.

The Church, he said, needed a mixture of conservative and radical; of heir and critic. Churches do change, but such change is done by development and re-emphasis, and not by repudiation.

He hoped the bishops would listen to the debate in such a way that they were able to fulfil their office.

These thunderbolts unleashed, Dr Runcie sat down. All eyes turned to the Bishop of Durham. He ran a few checks on himself for brimstone damage. He pushed his hands through his white hair: all clear. He took off his halfmoon specs and rubbed his eyes; no problem. He looked as healthy as York Minster before the fire.

Away from the Synod those who had opposed David Jenkins' consecration had not allowed the matter rest. The pressure group 'Action for Biblical Witness to our Nation' carried out its own survey to determine the views of bishops. Diocesan and suffragan bishops were asked three questions: Do you believe in the virgin birth of Christ as an historical event? Do you believe it is necessary for a Christian to believe in the incarnation of Christ as 'God made flesh'? Do you believe in the bodily resurrection of Christ from the tomb on the third day? Replies were received from 33 diocesan bishops (out of 44 contacted), 27 suffragan bishops (out of 62 contacted). Not all bishops replied to the specific questions, but of those who did 60 per cent stated they believed in the virgin birth as an historical fact and 63 per cent believed in the bodily resurrection of Christ. 45 per cent of diocesan bishops and 15 per cent of suffragan said they would allow bishops to hold the same views as the Bishop of Durham. 37 per cent of all bishops replying to the specific questions stated it was necessary to believe that Christ is 'God made flesh'.

The answers to the questions were published by A.B.W.O.N. giving each bishop's own view. The Bishop of Newcastle, for instance, wrote, 'Virgin birth does indeed imply precise historical fact but there are those among us who, whilst doubtful about the historical truth of the virgin birth, are convinced about its theological truth. Do we consider this option to be untenable in our Church?'

The Bishop of Guildford's reply was on these lines: 'I believe that God could have intervened in the normal course of nature and generated a child in the womb of Mary; whether he did so or not is now extremely difficult to detect and not of any great importance.'

According to the A.B.W.O.N. survey the following bishops in office in the latter part of 1984 answered all three questions positively: Aston, Burnley Bradford, Canterbury, Chester, Birkenhead, Chichester, Crediton, Croydon, Doncaster, Norwich, Plymouth, St Albans, St Edmundsbury and Ipswich, Sodor and Man, Thetford. In addition the following bishops stated they believed in both the virgin birth and the bodily resurrection as historical facts. Those above plus Bradwell, Chelmsford, Derby, Dover, Liverpool, Oxford, Peterborough, Pontefract, Reading, Salisbury, Sheffield, Shrewsbury, Wakefield.

The fact that a bishop does not appear in either list should not be taken necessarily to mean that he disbelieves the virgin birth or resurrection stories.

There were eighteen bishops who said they would allow fellow bishops to hold the same views as David Jenkins of Durham: Bradwell, Canterbury, Chelmsford, Derby, Dover, Ely, Gloucester, Guildford, Lancaster, Liverpool, Maidstone, Manchester, Newcastle, Salisbury, Southwark, Winchester, Worcester, York.

By April 1985, as well as completing the survey, A.B.W.O.N. had a petition with the signatures of 20,000 Anglican communicants to present to the Archbishop of Canterbury asking that in future those appointed Bishop should believe in the virgin birth and bodily resurrection of Christ as historical events, and in the necessity for a Christian to believe that Christ is 'God made flesh'. A.B.W.O.N. also had over one thousand parish clergy on its mailing list and declared three main aims and three current concerns.

The aims were 'prayerfully and in the power of the Holy Spirit':

1. To urge (a) proclamation of the biblical Gospel by the Church of England to the nation; (b) proclamation of biblical morality by the Church of England to the nation by word and example; (c) correction of unbiblical theology and morality within the Church of England through charitable, private or public action.

2. To give prayer, practical and moral support to those of whatever tradition who act on these aims.

3. To offer help to those who have fallen into error.

Current concerns include:

1. Urging the appointment as bishops and clergy only of those who privately believe and publicly affirm the Creeds as the Church has consistently interpreted them, and in particular believe in the virgin birth and bodily resurrection of Christ as 'historical events', and the necessity for a Christian to believe in the incarnation of Christ as 'God made flesh'.

2. Upholding the divinity of Christ and his uniqueness as the only way of salvation in all discussions of other faiths.

3. Proclaiming the biblical teaching that homosexual practices and adultery are sinful, whilst encouraging a compassionate approach to those tempted in these areas.

A.B.W.O.N. was gradually widening its concerns and

becoming another general evangelical pressure group. David Jenkins' answer to those in the evangelical camp who had expressed the greatest reservations about his bishopric came in the form of a sermon entitled 'Fundamentalism Fundamentally Flawed'. He began by repeating the claim that 'we cannot define, describe, evaluate or pin down God. This must be so for God is God; and if he is not beyond us, about us and beyond our grasp, he is simply one of us – one thing among the things with which we can cope – in which case he is not God'. He talked too of the inadequacy of human language.

'In logic, language cannot be adequate for God. He cannot be contained by any of the descriptions which we try to give of him, or by any of the stories which we are authorized to tell of him. Take a miracle. If we know exactly what it is and precisely how it works it ceases to be a miracle, and it cannot be termed a miracle, a wonder speaking of God; without faith a miracle is not perceived as such. Take the resurrection; scan the records in detail and you will find again and again there is room for doubt, for personal apprehension, and, above all, for interpretation. God, when he acts in the salvation of the world cannot be pinned down and cannot be discerned without a responsive faith.'

David Jenkins took the word 'father' as an example. Take it literally, he said, and there may be little short of hell to pay. Again with the Trinity, he suggested. It was a glorious symbol of ultimate truth but not to be understood too precisely or all sorts of complications would ensue.

He then moved away from language to the subject of contemplation and how God could be experienced. But the experience he warned was not to be grabbed at and analysed or examined. God is no object of critical investigation but the subject of faith and hope, of obedience, of love and of longing.

How did this approach square with David Jenkins' work as an academic, a questioner? The idea, he said, that as a professor he was allowed to ask the awkward questions but as a bishop he was not, struck him as appalling, almost blasphemous.

'Surely, theology is something which has to be pursued with the utmost academic vigour and the utmost academic devotion. No questions can be barred. But this is made possible and required by the very giving and the very being of God. It is God himself who compels us to the critical pursuit of truth with integrity and to face every question possible.

'Christian theology, however, even as an academic discipline, cannot avoid being in some real sense confessional, for without the confession of Jesus as Lord, which expands into the confession and praise of the Holy Trinity, God the Father, God the Son and God the Holy Spirit, there would be no subject matter for the disciplines that make up academic theology. Similarly, Christian theology, even as an academic discipline, cannot avoid retaining or regaining some sense of the contemplative and continuing: awareness of God, of the Divine, of the Holy, of the Mysterious. For without at least a claim to such a search or such an awareness, the disciplines of Christian theology would have no deposit or subject matter to study. That is why such a theologian as Anselm (like such a composer as Haydn) could not get down to his work without prayer. Without some imaginative sympathy with the contemplative, no one could expect to appreciate what the deposits of Christian faith, life and Church are the deposits of and are the deposits for.

'Thus, even as a set of academic disciplines, in a secular university, in a secular world, Christian theology must retain something of the confessional and something of the contemplative. But there is no contradiction between the requirements of this and the requirements of academic

166

integrity and freedom – quite the contrary. For the God who is confessed is not afraid of facts, and the God who is glimpsed in contemplation is freedom, openness and listening. God is no shadowy illusion and neither is his world, for he has created it and he has invested his purposes in it. Further, as we Christians are aware, in the pursuit of his purposes he has become one of the created beings in it, and poured his spirit into men and women in order to further and consummate his creation, his purposes and his incarnation.

'Thus, while there is struggle, and even suffering, both in the practice und in the process of bringing together the confessional, the devotional, and the critical, there is no contradiction either basically or in the end between the critical questioning mind and the devout, obedient spirit – no contradiction whatever when all is related to the true God and Father of Our Lord Jesus Christ. God demands both, and God requires and offers the consummation of both in an ultimate unity of reality, truth and love, which utterly transcends and wholly fulfils them both.

'As Augustine says at the end of his twenty-two books on the "City of God" – "There we shall be still and see; we shall see and we shall trust; we shall love and we shall praise. Behold what will be that end without end, for what is our end but to reach that Kingdom that has no end." (*De civ. dei* XXII. 30)

'But, meanwhile, we have to serve the Kingdom, to wait for the Kingdom and to witness to the Kingdom. Until that Kingdom comes, and as part of the coming of the Kingdom, we have to take absolutely seriously (although not absolutely, for only God is to be taken absolutely – not even our ideas of God, but only God himself) all that has developed in the history of the world and in the searching of the human spirit. The God whom the prophets of Israel could recognize as active in Cyrus cannot have ceased his prophetic, creative and redemptive activities in history at the end of the biblical era; although some people seem to think that God switched off at approximately A.D. 90, flashed on round about Luther and has switched off ever since. What sort of God is this who is absent from most of the history of the world? Not the biblical one, not the God and Father of our Lord Jesus Christ.

'When the God-given minds of men and women (created in the image of God) develop the explorations, experiments and critical methods of science, of history, of social critiques, and psychological investigations, they may, of course, put these things to false and dangerous uses, but we cannot doubt that God meant them to be developed or we are doubting his wisdom, his presence and his power. So we are bound to bring, both to the academic study of theology, and to common-sense development of a living Christian faith, all the resources which science, history, sociology and psychology make available to us. Of course, we must seek to use these immense and exciting resources of the critical mind in relation to the worship and humility of the devout and obedient spirit. But in so doing, we must be very careful that we do not substitute obscuranticism for devotion and claim mysteries where we will not confront muddles. Our God must be the God of truth, and he cannot be served by any pretences whatever. If, in fact, we pretend – in the face, for instance, of careful comparison of the text of the Gospel of Mark with the text of the Gospels of Luke and Matthew – that it is still possible to hold that every word of the Bible is directly dictated by God, then we are cheating and so in effect, blaspheming against the God who is truth. For such a comparison shows that Luke and Matthew are prepared to exercise free rewriting on Mark. So we must be clear that the Bible is a human book, witnessing to God by the Spirit of God through human means and human errors, as well as human insights. To continue a pretence about some special, magical, super-natural guarantee of the very words of the Bible is to deny God in history, and reject his use of the human, and to invite the Rationalist Press Association to feel fully justified in regarding all religion as outmoded superstition.

'Similarly, the claims of the Church and the churches have to be subjected to all the valid insights of a Marx or a Freud or a Dürkheim. It is as plain as a pikestaff, as Marx said, that religion is again and again used in the interests of the ruling classes (for example when it is not, there is trouble in *The Daily Telegraph*). Freud, and his followers and critics have many valid insights, for instance about projection and dependency which make people want a comforting, father-figure bishop and not a disturbing apostolic one! Dürkheim has provocative and revealing questions about the whole business of religion as a social bond, so that we are not really concerned about God but about keeping our society and morals together. Ideologies and doctrines of man built up solely upon a Marx or a Freud or a Dürkheim have, of course, to be persistently and resolutely challenged, but this has to be done with a proper use of, and a proper respect for, what a Marx or a Freud or a Dürkheim has brought into our understanding of human history and of our behaviour, corporate and individual. Once a valid question has been raised, there is no going back on it, if you believe in God. There is only going forward from it.

'Thus, as God is the God of history and as God has created us in his image, the critical use of all the tools of human reason and study which are required for academic integrity are also required of us for a simple and basic theological reason, the being and giving of God. One of the main contributions, therefore, that real faith in God and serious theology ought to make to our present confusions and conflicts is to support us in refusing to accept any orthodoxies, any theologies, any dogmatic acceptance of theories political, economic or psychological, which shut up men and women in anything less than God. Theology should be at the heart of all academic integrity and criticism and exploration, because of the being and giving of God.

'Let me add to this two footnotes – two footnotes, of course, which ought to be developed into chapters 2 and 3, but there is not time to go on much longer! First, the full use of the critical mind in relation to the devout spirit is required by the very mystery of God – the mystery from which I started this sermon. Of course, theology, faith and practice, at all levels, must again and again be criticized by all the resources we have can use. Otherwise how do we perceive and challenge the errors, the superstitions and the frequent littleness of actual faith, together with the perpetual tendency of all religious people and all religious systems to be more concerned with "my" or "our" religion, its beliefs, its formulae and its practices, rather than with the living God. As one of my numerous correspondents said recently, there is an awful lot of religion about, but very little spirituality. As many people take up religion to hide from God as to get closer to him. More positively, surely we must use all critical resources available to us, so that we may again and again break open our perceived images and practices and beliefs so that the glory of God may be released, or rather that we may be released on our pilgrimage towards that glory.

'Secondly, and finally, it may be said – it is often said – "But this is impossibly risky". How can we be sure if anything and everything can be and sometimes must be criticized? The beginnings of a positive but disturbing answer to this disturbing question lie, I believe, in two points, and the first is this. We cannot be sure unless God gives us assurance to which we respond in discipleship and pilgrimage so that we grow in the knowledge of him. Growth in the knowledge of God, as all the saints have known, is growth into the unknown, sometimes through knowing and being known and then into the dark night, and then out again into the light and then through and on again. But we cannot be sure. It is only God who can give us himself – nothing whatsoever in this world guarantees God; but God gives himself.

170

'The second thing is this – and this may perhaps be in some ways the most difficult thing I have to say, but I come increasingly to think that it is almost the most important. Yes, it is risky, and so is creation. If God has chosen to work by guaranteeing us some certain knowledge, delivered by certain means, which always work, then why does he not work like that in the world at large? But in the world at large, as in ourselves, we are faced with much evil, and much that is wholly and even devastatingly problematical. God must therefore take great risks. Otherwise his permitting, tolerating, taking on board, and having to do with evil is intolerable. If God has committed himself to the sort of safe policies of manipulation, as some people say he has, then why on earth does he not manipulate for love? Such a God, I believe, is unbelievable in the world. Love has chosen to take much greater risks. The fundamental flaw of any sort of fundamentalism is that it assumes a God who guarantees and controls in detail much more than the world shows that he does.

'So a final reason why academic integrity, Christian devotion and Christian theology are wholly compatible is the risky nature of God's whole enterprise. This has the cross at the heart of it for an absolutely fundamental reason. The cross is the very expression of the reality and the power, and the promise of God. So we have to work with him with all the resources we have, and we can do this in hope, despite all the difficulties, all the threats, and all the errors, because we believe, and are sure, that God has committed himself to this risky world. He has been with us as Jesus, and he has been crucified for us, and he has risen up through risk. The Kingdom is not manipulated nor does it come by avoiding risk or by delivering absolute guarantees beyond risk. God calls us in Christ to take on these things, to suffer these things and to live these things for the sake and the certainty of the Kingdom. Academic integrity, properly pursued, like life, is full of risks, but we take them because they are responded to, and they can be redeemed by the grace of God, by the presence of God, and by the promise of God.'

David Jenkins has been accused by a fellow bishop of causing havoc. There have been numerous demands for his resignation, he has produced apoplectic rage in many an even-tempered priest, he has roused the anger of the Conservative party and been described as a heretic, as foolish and ill-informed, and a walking clerical disaster; although it should also be pointed out that he has had a profoundly liberating effect on many Christians who found that they were not required to believe certain things that they found incredible. However much he might have been surprised and even hurt by the initial reaction to the first 'Credo' programme, he had certainly never intended to be a quiet and uncontroversial figure as bishop.

When he was offered the See, his wife Mollie recalls, it was a difficult decision whether to accept or not. The deciding argument perhaps was this, 'You cannot say no if you have fought for the Church of England all your life. I told him that he had always preached about "God the disturber" and he could hardly say that he wasn't going to be disturbed – but he accepted with a deep sigh, quite honestly.'

And he found himself with a nation as a tutorial group. If the role of a don is to probe, provoke and even disturb students into producing their best ideas, he was not going to change that donnish technique just because his audience was larger and less well prepared.

David Jenkins does not despise those of simple faith but feels they are not fulfilling their potential. A simple faith is but a first step. God-given reason and one's whole intellectual capacity should be employed to test and strengthen faith at every stage of development.

What many of his opponents are now wondering is whether David Jenkins is under-estimating the strength and

172

value of simple faith and over-estimating the intellectual capabilities of the human race? As a professional disturber with ready access to a public platform, is he unnecessarily undermining the existing strengths of simple faith and not offering anything positive in return?

He argues that God could have produced a virgin birth but says he does not think this is the way God does things. In other words he is saying an historical virgin birth does not appear to be reasonable. He therefore produces a reasoned argument as to how the story could have come about, maintaining all the while a belief in the essential truth of the incarnation. If he is prepared to accept an omnipotent God who became an ordinary man one might ask why should the traditional method of his incarnation, the virgin birth be such a stumbling block? It could be that David Jenkins and other liberal theologians do not want to appear out of step with mainstream scientific and secular thought. That approach tends to overlook the fact that mainstream scientific thought is tending to move more and more away from the old, purely material and mechanistic view of the universe; that popular thought is now far more receptive to ideas beyond nature and, anyway, one could ask, should not a dedicated disturber be prepared to challenge scientific orthodoxy and not try to link in with it?

As it happened, the real disturbance has been felt by those whose own faith depends very heavily on a literal belief in the virgin birth and bodily resurrection. David Jenkins has asked them to consider how much more important is a belief in a living God, at work in the world today, than a belief in an historical event which cannot be proven in any ordinary way.

'It's about time,' David Jenkins said in *She* magazine in Feburary 1985,

> that people woke up to the way things really are, and the only way you can do that apparently is by going through some shocks that you would rather not have.

173

[On the virgin birth and resurrection] there are forty other bishops who have never said anything about it, at least not in a way that has made anybody listen.

I simply believe I'm not a heretic. The major heresy today, and it is a dangerous one, is saying you must interpret the Christian faith in the way that I, or my party insist, which is the very essence of heresies, of the choosing a distinctive thing about the faith and insisting on it.

People get fed up with my language, like 'conjuring tricks' or 'I wouldn't put it past God'. I'm sorry but its actually part of my theology. I think incarnation means that God, about whom you cannot be too reverent, or too mysterious, or in one way too afraid, has chosen to commit himself to the ordinariness. I mean he wasn't a special man when he was Jesus, he was an ordinary man. And I want to make it clear to people I wouldn't put it past God.

The only thing appropriate to God is silence. Silence in awe. Silence when I want to prostrate myself.

David Jenkins is both an unorthodox bishop and a traditional one. He lives in the labyrinthine Auckland Castle, though perhaps in a more simple style than many of his predecessors. Unlike many bishops past and present who have mastered the technique of being grand and aloof. David Jenkins enjoys meeting the ordinary people of the diocese. It is not unknown for him to pop into the back of an ordinary parish church as a member of the congregation for evensong. He likes what some bishops see as the chore of confirmation and preaching to ordinary congregations 'and trying to put them into the context of the love of God, and drawing things out of them. I love teaching people to say their prayers. I'm not very good at it myself, that's what makes me good at teaching it. I think.' At home, Auckland Castle has a chapel to which the bishop can retire. But David Jenkins describes the role of prayer in his life like this: 'Dropping in and out of prayer all over the place plays a big part in my life. I'm not one of those who gets up two hours early or anything to make sure. It's more a matter of recollection in the presence of God, or the recollection of God within you – the business of just watching what is going by, even when I am walking to the station.'

In many ways David Jenkins is a public figure manufactured by the curious processes of news selection adopted by the media today. Journalists found him good material with which to work. From their point of view there had been a vacancy for a controversial prelate at the time and David Jenkins' ability to produce the 'quotable quote' made him an ideal candidate for the position. It is a perilous position as ultimately, in order to get a platform, a public figure has to relinquish control over his words.

Theologically he is an orthodox liberal, and what he has said is not outrageous by the standards of lecture halls and seminar rooms. The fact that the Church of England has for so long been a broad and tolerant Church, prepared to embrace both liberal and traditional theologians, provided no one made too much of an issue of the differences in public, had resulted in a gap developing between the complex theology of academics and the simplified preaching received by the faithful in the pews. David Jenkins feels the gap is one of dishonesty. By use of the provocative and quotable phrase he has single-handed brought the complexities of modern liberal theology out into the open. He has said that ordinary people can and should consider the latest thinking.

In doing so he has opened a wound in the Church, a wound which existed previously but was covered up. He has knowingly disturbed the peace. The consequences are beyond his control.

Postscript

Now that the tumult and the shouting aroused by the Bishop of Durham's remarks on the virgin birth and the resurrection have begun to die away, it should be possible to discern the real issues of the controversy. So much misquotation and misunderstanding, and so much immoderate passion, have clouded the atmosphere until recently that a balanced judgement has been very difficult. Ted Harrison has now set out here what was actually said and written, and the events which took place.

This book may have unwittingly given the impression that the Jenkins debate was purely an Anglican affair, to be dealt with and if possible settled within the confines of the Church of England. But the doctrines of the Christian faith are the concern of all Christians. The Church of England contains only a certain proportion of the Christians in this country, and the other churches, the Church of Scotland, the Roman Catholic Church and the Free Churches, are also, with the Church of England, the guardians and expounders of the faith. Thus they are vitally involved.

Yet the non-Anglican Churches have taken the whole matter much more calmly than the Church of England. The Methodist Conference of 1985, for instance (containing people with views just as contradictory to each other as those of David Jenkins and David Holloway), welcomed 'the openness and honesty of the Bishop of Durham in recent theological statements, and is encouraged by the opportunity for a wider public discussion of the Christian faith'.

It could be that, wrongly, non-Anglicans have not wanted to intrude on Anglican preserves, or that, at least in some cases, they have already come to terms with issues which have, after all, been in the Church's knowledge for a long time.

But, of course, the Church of England has also been fully engaged with these issues, often in the books of very notable scholars, ever since the rise of biblical criticism. William Temple, afterwards Archbishop of Canterbury, and acknowleged unofficial leader of the whole church in this country, was troubled – and troubled others – at the time of his ordination in 1909, by doubts about the virgin birth and the physical resurrection of Jesus; and Ted Harrison has described above the difficulties of Bishop Hensley Henson in 1918.

Why then the great furore? Partly because of the media, without a doubt; partly because of the 'bishop factor': what a bishop says is more newsworthy and more provocative than the same thing said a hundred times before by others; partly because of this particular bishop's personality; but also because, as it must be feared, the Anglican people have not been let fully into the confidence of the clergy, who have known about these problems since their college days.

This is not, of course, to say that the bishop is wholly right and his critics wholly wrong in this controversy, or vice versa; but only that the matter would have been dealt with more peaceably, if there had been greater education of the people in the past, and less hysteria in the present.

But one suggestion made by some (only some) of David Jenkins' critics must be ruled out of court at the start; that the burning of York Minster was God's punishment of the Church for Jenkins' consecration. This suggestion is wholly out of accord with all that Jesus teaches about God, whose miracles are miracles of mercy and not of destruction. Natural disasters may be mysterious, but they are not God's vengeance. We can be sure that lightning would have struck the south transept at York whether Jenkins had been consecrated there or not.

But other questions are not so easy to answer. On the virgin birth we may begin by giving the scriptural evidence. The virgin birth (or, more accurately the virginal conception) is described in the first two chapters of St Matthew's Gospel and in the first two chapters of St Luke's Gospel. Nowhere else in the New Testament is it stated or alluded to. In both of these Gospels (in ch. 1 of Matthew and ch. 2 of Luke), there is evidence that some Christians contemporary with the Gospels did not believe in the virgin birth. This is in the form of genealogies of Jesus, one of them (in Matthew) from Abraham, the other (in Luke) from Adam, different in detail from each other, but each of them tracing the descent of Joseph, not Mary – and Joseph's descent is quite irrelevant if he was not the father of Jesus.

You can argue from this evidence that since Mary's virginity is asserted in two books of the Bible, the silence of the other books does not matter. And the genealogies may have been drawn up by those who did not know the facts. The widespread ignorance of Mary's virginal conception can be explained by supposing that Mary did not reveal it until late in her life.

On the other hand, it has often been pointed out that the narratives surrounding the birth of Jesus in both Matthew and Luke have an atmosphere quite different from that of the rest of the Gospels. They are told in the manner of folk-stories which have been handed round and down by Christians several decades after the events which they describe, and incorporated by Matthew and Luke into their Gospels more or less as they stood.

Thus the scriptural evidence is inconclusive, and it will surely be admitted that for an event so startling as a virgin

179

birth particularly strong evidence is required. This is not forthcoming. Thus no one really ought to say that the virgin birth is historically demonstrated, even if it is to be believed on other grounds.

Whether we believe it to be a historical fact or not probably depends on our theological position. The virgin birth itself cannot determine that position, since it cannot itself be demonstrated. In any case Christian faith is not believing that certain things happened, even a miraculous virgin birth. Christian faith, though of course it is directed and inspired by events which are believed to have happened, and especially by the birth, death and resurrection of Jesus, is not *in an historical event*, but in Jesus Christ the person.

Some people are helped to believe in Jesus by accepting the evidence that he was born of a virgin; they believe that his position as Son of God is safeguarded, even proved, by this.

Others hold a quite different view. If the Son of God truly became a man, he must surely have become *fully* a man; a virginal birth would put him outside the category and experience of human beings. We should have no chance of being really like him, since he would have advantages that we do not possess. The Christian doctrine of the incarnation, therefore, does not require a virgin birth; in fact, it tends to be obscured by it. And it is certain that Paul and John, in many ways the architects of Christian doctrine, carried out their work without taking any account of a virgin birth at all.

Thus those Christians who, like Bishop Jenkins, doubt whether Jesus was born of a virgin, hold just as strong a faith in Jesus Christ, the incarnate Son of God, as those with no such doubts. Belief in a historical virgin birth cannot be said to be an essential part of Christian faith.

Another misunderstanding needs to be cleared up. Christians who do not accept the historical occurrence of the virgin birth are not saying that the birth stories in Matthew and Luke are untrue. They are saying that they are *myths* – in the proper sense of that much misused word. A myth is a story told (which may or may not be historically accurate) to express a truth which is beyond exact, literal, scientific exposition. It uses language akin to that of poetry. The birth stories are myths which express the mysterious truth that Jesus, the eternal Son of God, entered human life as a man.

How then did stories first told as myths become widely accepted as facts? There was the prophecy in Isaiah which said: 'A virgin shall conceive' – though we now know that what Isaiah wrote in Hebrew was: 'A young woman shall conceive'. It was held by many in the early Church – though not, as far as we know, by Jesus himself – that a virgin is a purer, more honourable woman than one who has taken part in sexual intercourse with a husband. This notion was strengthened by the ideas of some who came into the Church from pagan religions which held the sexual act to be in itself shameful. Mary because of her obedience to God and her privileged position as mother of Jesus came to be honoured more and more. It was very natural as that process went on to suppose that she must have been a virgin, to accept the birth stories as literally true, and to insert the virgin birth into the Creed.

The case of the resurrection of Christ is different. Here we touch the nerve centre of Christian faith. The New Testament is in large measure focussed upon the resurrection; and Christians claim to have a direct personal experience, in the eucharist and at other times, of the power and presence of the living Christ. Most of them would echo Paul's words: 'If Christ is not raised, our faith is vain'.

It is beyond doubt that David Jenkins wounded the deep sensitivities of many Christians by denying, or virtually denying, that God raised the body of Jesus alive from the tomb. The picture of Jesus emerging from the grave in glorious triumph, visibly and tangibly, to the consternation of his enemies and the rejoicing of his friends, has been inscribed on the Christian imagination from very early times. It has the authority of the Gospels, it appears and reappears in art and literature, it is enshrined in innumerable liturgies and prayers and hymns. To cast doubt on it seemed to throw the freezing waters of rationalism over the dearest beliefs of Christians down the ages. It is not altogether surprising that there was an angry and pained reaction.

But sober reflection will show that David Jenkins was not destroying faith in the resurrection. He was bringing into the open a fact well known to scholars for many years, that the New Testament narratives of the resurrection are inconsistent with each other; and in particular that the earliest and therefore the most authoritative narrative of all, by many years, that of Paul in the First Letter to the Corinthians (ch. 15), makes no mention of the empty tomb at any point, but speaks only of the numerous occasions when the risen Jesus made himself known to his friends.

And he invites us to look at Paul's narrative, which the apostle claims to have received from the leaders of the Church in Jerusalem, more closely. Paul recounts how on various occasions Jesus appeared to Peter, to the apostles as a body, to five hundred Christians assembled together, to James his own brother – and then to Paul himself. Now it is clear that the appearance to Paul could not have been physical even on the traditional view, since it took place after the ascension. Why then on the traditional view is it mentioned by Paul in the same breath as the appearances that *were* physical? It begins to look as if Paul did not hold the traditional view; that he did not suppose *any* of the appearances to be physical. And this impression is strongly confirmed by the absence of reference to the emptiness of the tomb, and by his forthright statement in the same chapter that 'flesh and blood shall not inherit the kingdom of God'.

The matter is made difficult for modern readers by the change in meaning of the word 'body' since the time of Paul. We think of the body as a physical structure; he thought of it as the total self, composed of flesh, soul and spirit. When he comes, still in the same chapter, to describe the resurrection of those who believe in Christ, he speaks of a 'spiritual body', continuous with and developed out of our present body, but different from it, and not containing flesh and blood. He may well have thought of the risen Jesus in the same way; certainly his whole emphasis is on the *person* of Jesus making himself known to his friends, and physical factors play no part at all in the description of the risen Christ.

So Paul asserted the personal resurrection of Jesus, God's raising of Jesus from the dead, without any reference to his physical body or his emergence from the tomb (of which, indeed, he may never have heard). David Jenkins asserts the personal resurrection of Jesus, his personal commission to his friends and his personal promise of power through the Holy Spirit, but does not see any need for believing that the tomb was empty on Easter Day. Jenkins can justly claim that his gospel of the resurrection is essentially the same as Paul's. He certainly cannot be justly accused of denying the resurrection.

Many people, in spite of all this, will still prefer to accept the stories of the empty tomb quite literally, and then they will have to try to harmonize them with each other and with Paul's account. Others will prefer David Jenkins' approach; they will have no difficulty in recognizing the gospel stories as myths, in the sense given above, and as myths which were asserted as facts after the destruction of Jerusalem in 70 AD made it impossible to check their accuracy.

Yet in either case, though the process has been painful for many, surely it can now be seen that by provoking the serious discussion of issues which are important for every

183

Christian, Bishop Jenkins has done good and not harm to the Church at large.

RUPERT E. DAVIES
*Former President of the Methodist Conference
and formerly Principal of Wesley College,
Bristol*